Sedona Mountain Biking:
The Rise of the Gnarly Crew

By Ramajon
www.sedonamountainbiking.net

This Book is Dedicated to My Buddy
MAXDOG

I would also like to thank THE NOD who created more logos and art work than any bike shop deserved to have

Last but not least, I would like to thank Tom Bird who helped me let go of my distractions which allowed me to follow my dreams and actually write this first of many books

I LOVE YOU, PLEASE FORGIVE ME,
THANK YOU, I'M SORRY

Ho'oponpono
Words of the Wise

Copyright © 2013 by Ramajon

All rights reserved.

Cover design by ciejay Gear
Book design by Ramajon

No part of this book may be reproduced in any form or by any electronic or mechanical means including information storage and retrieval systems, without permission in writing from the author. The only exception is by a reviewer, who may quote short excerpts in a review.

A Bikeapelli Press, LLC Book, Published by Lightning Source, a subsidiary of Ingram Press Publishers

Bikeapelli Press, LLC Books are available through Ingram Press, and available for order through Ingram Press Catalogues

This book is a work of fiction. Names, characters, places, and incidents either are products of the author's imagination or are used fictitiously. Any resemblance to actual persons, living or dead, events, or locales is entirely coincidental.

Ramajon

Visit my website at www.sedonamountainbiking.net

Printed in the United States of America

First Printing: November 2012
Bikeapelli Press, LLC

ISBN: 978-1-627-47004-9
Ebook ISBN: 978-1-625-17111-5
LCN: Pending

DISCLAIMER

Due to the extremely controversial nature of mountain biking, especially in the overcharged political atmosphere of Sedona, I have decided to include this disclaimer.

This is a story about a fictitious sport in a fictitious land named Sedona.

The characters are not intended to represent real people, and the acts attributed to the characters never happened.

The only truth in this book is about the family spirit that developed in Sedona amongst the Mountain Bike Heaven community . . .

and

How the forest service neglected their responsibility for decades to accommodate this extremely fast-growing user group.

FOREWORD

The mountain bike community that grew up around Mountain Bike Heaven became my family. I attracted each and every one of the riders for one reason or another and they all became a reflection of some part of me. Over the years, I felt very much like a circus ringleader, a mountain bike circus ringleader. Or, perhaps like a mad scientist who invented a mountain bike Frankenstein, because once it got started, it became a monster that no one could control. The one overriding concept was that each rider lived to ride and rode to live. We all have our personal struggles in life and career and family, but once we jump on those mountain bikes, life's troubles and hardships fade into the background and are soon left far behind. The beauty of the club rides was that there were no judgments, except the ones we put on ourselves. We may have been competitive when we rode, but we were all there to have fun, put life's problems behind and get our "ya yas" out. For most of us, mountain biking became our spiritual lifeblood, and that was the commonality that ran through us all and helped us connect with nature and become the Sedona mountain bike family. Our success was that we were out there riding and no matter how screwed up the rest of the world was, it didn't matter one bit to us, at least until we broke something or the ride was over.

IN THE BEGINNING

Coming to Sedona was a magical experience. Sedona was the heart of the new age, and I had been the heart of the new age in my health food store, Rising Sun Natural Foods. Now I was going to be with others who were drawn here just like me. This wasn't my plan; it was the cosmic plan. Who knew what would be the outcome—certainly not me. I had been on a spiritual quest for so long, and now again a new place, a new move, a new adventure. The road less traveled was where I was and I was right at home. I arrived with all my belongings in my Toyota Tercel wagon with two bikes on the roof. I had given up my health food store in Cleveland Heights, and now I was on a new adventure . . . just what it was to be I had no clue, but I was young and full of passion and ready for the unknown. I was here to see what I would see and I hadn't a clue of what that was to be. There were new faces and new adventures awaiting me, and I was once again alone and ready to find myself again.

Immediately it was clear that my experience upon arrival was just like everyone else's. We were all drawn to Sedona for some greater purpose. Most wanted to set up a new age or health center. Not I; I was here for something else. I hung with the New Agers, a conglomeration of UFO spotters and Native American shaman, charlatans, and con men. What the fuck was I doing here? I came through Hopi-land and caught a reggae show on the Second Mesa, a very befitting beginning, then, through Flagstaff, and the most amazing drive down Oak Creek Canyon. Who would have thought you could put a road through a canyon like that? I was in total awe and my jaw was open the whole drive down the Canyon as I stared in disbelief at the huge cliffs and spires and colors. Then when Sedona appeared out of the bottom of the Canyon and those magnificent red rocks came into view, I was in love.

First stop, Food Among the Flowers, the only vegetarian restaurant in town. It was run by a batty seventy-two-year-old gal named Doris. Doris had big plans and she taught me how to make omelets during the first week of my Sedona adventure. She was working out of a converted garage and attracted the cream of the crop of Sedona's New Age crazies. One of my favorites was a comedian named Tony Sills, who would start to get funny after four or five cups of coffee. I can't remember any of his jokes now. I just remember that he had all of us rolling with laughter. There was also this gal who worked in the kitchen, and every time she spoke, I would turn around expecting to see someone I knew. It took me a while to figure that one out. It turned out that she was from Ohio, which was where I had just come from, and her voice intonations where the same as the ones I had been listening to for the past five years. Or, perhaps I knew her from a past life. At any rate, it turned out she was to be my first Sedona love, and boy was that a love to remember. She was the only other person who showed up in town with two bikes, a road bike and a mountain bike. We were to be some of Sedona's earliest mountain bikers. There were others, but we liked to think that we were the first, kind of like the Adam and Eve of the Sedona mountain bike community.

Why a bike shop in the first place? Besides the fact that Sedona has great trails and the town was itching for something new, it seemed to be my destiny. Most of all, Sedona was missing something to bring people together in the red rocks that was both physical and active and full of adventure. I received my divine inspiration from Bikapelli, the primordial mountain biker who has transcended our universe and now rides within us all. And, I was in the right place at the right time with the right vision. The New Agers were way too into their heads for me, and the artists were just too artsy. I guess the only thing left for me was something really physical, and that turned out to be mountain biking. For me it was a natural, and it became one of my spiritual practices. With mountain biking, you needed to get through the form of learning to ride to get to the essence of riding the flow, or as we said years later, "surfing the geological wave." Tapping into this flow became our religion, and Mountain Bike Heaven became our church, and the club rides became our Sunday services. Mountain biking took the place of a religion for most of us, and we literally pedaled ourselves to nirvana on the club rides. Of course, in those days the sacred herb was a big part of riding and we stopped often to catch our breath, or was that to breathe that special smoke. There is something about smoking herb and riding mountain bikes that pervaded the timelessness of Sedona's red rocks. Maybe we'd done this before with the peace pipe or something. I don't know, but it just went hand in hand for many us.

There are other similarities between a spiritual practice and mountain biking. It becomes a compulsion. For many mountain bikers, if they don't get out on their bikes and ride, they feel totally out of sorts. Sometimes it takes a moment or two to figure out what is wrong, but then the light bulb goes off, and we realize that our mountain bike is there waiting in a forgotten corner, and it's time to hop on board and pedal ourselves to oblivion. Becoming one with our bike and surroundings is one of the simplest ways to achieve balance and harmony and is much like a yoga or tai chi. It's quite obvious that by watching the way we approach our riding, we can gain great insight into our learning and spiritual process. What really keeps us riding isn't the physical aspects, but the spiritual ones. Every ride is like a new day, a new adventure, and each ride might just be the best ride of the year. Our mental and physical attitudes easily change as we pedal, and I know more than a few mountain bikers who would be a danger to themselves and society as a whole, if they didn't get out and pedal. There is probably a scientific explanation for all of this related to endorphins or oxygenation of the blood, but in reality it is more likely explained by the fun factor quotient. It is just so much darn fun out there pedaling, that we have all become addicted to it.

At first we rode the dirt roads out by Long Canyon, the heart of the UFO country and home of secret bases of the Men in Black. Then we progressed to Dead Man's Pass and the Coxcomb trails. Those early rides were always an adventure, and some times we would get lost in the process. My first experience was one of riding my bike in Boynton Canyon and then locking my bike to a tree. My bike was green and locking it to a green tree was not the brightest thing I ever did, but when your new to Sedona things like that seem to happen. Lucky for me, I made a point of looking at a particular view of the canyon as I walked away from my bike. When I returned from my hike-about, I could not find my bike. I was beginning to panic until I remembered the view and as I looked around for that view, I literally backed into my bike.

The first time Cindy, the gal from the restaurant, and I rode from the Little Elf trailhead, we were heading towards the caves up on Coffee Pot Rock. We parked our bikes and then went hiking up to the caves. This time I thought I had learned my lesson and I made a point of marking our walk from the bikes to the caves with small rock cairns. But as far as marking our way out of the woods from the bikes, I wasn't that smart. It had gotten dark as we got back to our bikes, so riding out was out of the question. We trudged around in the dark for what seemed like an eternity, but was probably only several hours, until we found our way out through someone's backyard. That day we were saved by one of the many social trails that the forest circus would grow to hate. In those days, Sedona rolled up the sidewalks at dark, some things never change, and we wanted to reward ourselves with a nice meal for actually finding our way out of the woods unscathed. The only restaurant open was Phil and Eddie's Diner, now called the Red Planet Diner, but in those days was referred to as the Caffeine and Tobacco Diner. The only thing that appeared edible on the menu was a tuna salad sandwich on white bread. We braved our better judgment, had the sandwich, and survived to ride another day.

Another early adventure with Cindy was on the Lower Loop horse trails. I had just discovered the area a few days earlier and had met Old Man Schuerman, and I had given the old cowboy a crystal as thanks for showing me where to park. I don't think he had ever seen a crystal, or a mountain biker for that matter. And I doubt he knew what to do with either of them. But, then again, I'm not sure I knew what to do with a crystal, at least not Sedona-style. That first day as I headed down the 9845 dirt road, I was led by a bald eagle and was amazed as the big views of Oak Creek opened up before my eyes. I couldn't wait to show Cindy the new ride area I had found. On that ride with Cindy a few days later, we tried some of the many single tracks that the horse people had laid out years before, and guess what, we got lost again. This was beginning to become a pattern. Of course, Cindy had to get to work at the Oak Creek Owl, one of Sedona's finest restaurants in those days, so it became quite a stressed-out challenge to find our way back to the car. But, this time we made it out before dark, again unscathed, and Cindy made it to work at the Owl without being late.

THE PARADE OF RIDERS BEGINS

The rides went on and, as we found more areas to ride and more trails, we also attracted more riders. One of the earliest mountain bike friends I attracted was Simon Bosman. Simon was from South Africa, had a bit of a stutter that made his accent even harder to understand, and had a total lack of fear. He is kind of a smallish guy but is fit as a fiddle. There are a lot of stories about Simon because he has done some amazing or amazingly stupid things over the years, and he was my first customer when I opened the bike shop. By then Mountain Bike Heaven was open and he showed up at the bike shop with a broken bike and a story of little ball bearings falling out of his freewheel at the top of Schnebly Hill. I knew there were bearings in a freewheel, but being a new mechanic, I never imagined that they would or could fall out. I never had anyone else show up with the same problem of little ball bearings falling out of their bike, but we have been plagued with freewheel and freehub body problems over the years. I guess that's just one of those under-built parts that bike manufacturers are notorious for building, or it could be Sedona.

I soon found out that Simon was tough on his bike and had quite a disregard for taking care of it. When I looked at his bike that first time, the freewheel was only one of the many problems. I couldn't figure out how his bike even worked. I did know that the loose hubs and super wobbly wheels and the cracks in his upper and lower headset crowns made his bike unsafe to ride. But, as I rode bikes with Simon over the years, I realized that these were only minor problems for Simon and his bikes. Years later, I asked him how many bike frames he broke, and after a moment of deep thought, he responded by saying, "All of them." When I sold him my Raleigh Peak demo bike, he put it through its paces on the first ride. We were just about to finish a ride out at Broken Arrow and Simon was way ahead. When I caught up to him, he was lying on the ground having rolled both of the tires off of the rims. I was just in time to watch both of his inner tubes expand out from under the tires and explode. We looked at each other in disbelief. I've never seen that happen again, but I have had to repair Simon's bike many times and have scratched my head in wonderment on more than a few occasions. Simon and I went on to ride many rides together, and you know what, he really did break all his bikes over and over and over again.

Simon has the honor of being one of the earliest known mountain bikers to sit in a prickly pear cactus. We all have had encounters with cactus, and some riders have even lived to tell their tale. In Simon's case, it occurred on the old airport trail long before it was rerouted to end on Brewer Road. It was so bad that he had to have his girlfriend remove cactus needles from his backside, or in Simon's own words, "his ball sack." For a brief time after that incident, Simon was known as Stickum, but that nickname never stuck.

Simon and his brother, Chris, have always worked together at some sort of construction, physical labor sort of work. They are both bald, perhaps not by choice, and look like twins except that Chris is hulkingly muscular. Next to him, Simon looks delicate, but when he rides his bike, Simon is anything but delicate. Because of Simon's total lack of fear and love of speed, we knew he could win downhill races and told him so over and over. One year he acquiesced and raced the downhill circuit for a season. As we expected, he did well and became a national expert downhill champ. I have to tell you, it came with a price, which included some of the gnarliest high-speed crashes that one would ever want to do. On a few occasions, Simon even stunned himself, but people from South Africa are a different breed and he healed quickly and kept getting back on the bike and kept going downhill faster and faster. All those crashes may have knocked his brain a little loose as witnessed by his descent down the brewery stairs on his bike blindfolded, which was featured in our very first ever Sedona mountain bike video entitled *Dances with Rocks*. Simon is not one to learn from his mistakes, or he could simply be addicted to adrenaline. His next feat for the camera was a radical descent down the slag pile just outside of Jerome. The slag pile itself may not have been so bad, but at the bottom of it there was a twelve-foot drop and nowhere to bale. Of course, bike brakes didn't stand a chance of stopping him before that drop-off, and he had to figure out a graceful way to bale. Needless to say, it wasn't pretty, but he also didn't die or even really injure himself, which was a feat in itself. The camera always seems to bring out the stupid in mountain bikers, and Simon has performed his fair share of stupid antics for the sake of our entertainment. He has always had luck on his side and is still alive and riding today, and I wouldn't be the least bit surprised to hear he is planning a comeback to downhill racing. As he has said on more than one occasion, "I am addicted to speed, I am addicted to adrenaline, I am going downhill very fast, I am riding my bike!"

There were two early mechanics at Mountain Bike Heaven. Jeffrey Roth, soon to be the Bogus Dude, and Steve Smeeth, soon to earn the name of Crazy Steve for doing some stupid or foolish thing. Both of these guys were works of art and led me to believe that our biking community was beginning to form out of the misfits of society, and that meant a lot when you consider that Sedona is the largest outpatient mental care facility on the face of the planet. None of the early mechanics were particularly great mechanics, but neither was I, so we all got along and were able to fix most bikes from parts we found on the floor. Other early riders included Gnarly Nerak, which is Karen spelled backwards, and Scott Barry, whose early claim to fame was to have been on the *Gong Show*. Barry came up from Phoenix twice a week for the club rides and sometimes brought a friend named Sean, who was an auto-paint-and-body dude. I had hooked up with Barry before opening the bike shop through Bogus Dude. Boggie had found him through a 900 number, which he was using to collect excuses for a book that he never wrote. When he spent three hundred dollars for his first mountain bike, he said he couldn't believe he had spent that much money on a bike. Barry earned the name Snake on our first Moab trip and was sure going to get his money's worth out of that bike. A little known point of fact was that Snake, and many of us other early mountain bikers, rode the stairs at Broken Arrow before Simon did. It wasn't until Simon saw us ride those stairs that he realized a mountain bike could do those kinds of things, and then there was no stopping him.

Another early mountain biker was Eric, the Bullish Dude. Bullish Dude was the product of a law enforcement family.

His mom was the one who carried the gun. A true bleeding heart liberal, Bullish would give the shirt off his back if you needed help, but sometimes the universe would interject itself into the equation, and at that point you never knew what the outcome of Bullish help might be. As you may have guessed, Bullish is a big guy, and he is hell on mountain bikes. I first met him in the original 500–square-foot Mountain Bike Heaven, which barely had enough room for a Bullish Dude to fit inside. He came in with his beat-up Univega mountain bike, and I'm sure it had a broken chain or a busted derailleur, or a bent chainring, or a flat tire, or in Bullish's case, probably all of the above. I can't remember the specifics, but I have worked on his bike so many times over the years that I know the drill. It's a simple equation: Bullish was so much stronger than those early mountain bikes and parts that they simply did not stand a chance. He once told me about his four-wheeling philosophy of always being conscious of getting back home in one piece. For some reason that philosophy never filtered through to his mountain biking modus operandi. As the years went on, Bullish got much better at comprehending the limits of bike parts, but to this day he is plagued by drive train issues and flat tires. I truly don't believe that mountain bike manufacturers have a clue about the raw strength that mountain bikers possess when it comes to thrashing on a bike. They think we are all super skilled, balanced, and ride with finesse. Some riders are like that, but the riders in Sedona, especially in the early years, were far away from that mark and, if anything, were quite the opposite. Bullish Dude was the case in point. Bullish was so strong, that when he hit the ground during a bike crash, the ground and definitely the bike lost out.

In those days, Bullish Dude had quite a temper, and one day I happened to be looking across the street from the bike shop when I saw him through his bike in anger at the dumpster next to where he was living. Later that day he showed up at the bike shop, with a long face, complaining that someone had stolen his bike. I responded by saying, "What do you expect when you through your bike in anger?" He had to do a double take, and then realized I must have seen him in action.

In order to truly understand how tough Bullish is, I have told innocent tourists that Sedona's famous sinkhole named the Devil's Kitchen was made larger when he crashed nearby and the whole earth shook and a big chunk of rock fell off the side. Another classic Bullish anecdote is how he pulled a whole cooked chicken out of his pack in the middle of a Jack's Canyon ride. As I had mentioned, Bullish would give the shirt off his back to help anyone who asked, but I tell you he was best suited for demolition. After he had moved up to Flagstaff because he had already broken everything in Sedona worth breaking, he was helping out on a bike shop renovation project. This was before they knew about the power of the Bullish Dude up in Flagstaff. Needless to say, the railing on the stairway that needed work soon was in pieces on the floor, perhaps not what they really intended.

Other characters from the early days include Smoking John and Volt. Smoking John was on our first club ride. The Buddha Beach trail had been scoped out by Crazy Steve years before on his motorcycle. We used this trail often in the early days and may have been the first mountain bikers to ride it when we used it for that first club ride. Smoking John earned his nickname because he smoked just about anything just about any time. Volt was a study in gnarlyness. He was not content to just ride his mountain bike. When we would take our rest breaks, Volt would shoulder his mountain bike and run up the nearest hill or mountain making as much noise as he could. He would then wait until we were riding again and head down his latest conquest, crashing through the shrubbery to join us on the trail like he had been there the whole time.

Dangerous Dave was an early rider who grew up in the area and would come by every time he had a break from chiropractic school. Dangerous is like the little brother who I never had. He is one of the most entertaining mountain bikers, a natural athlete, and a chiropractor to boot who specializes in trailside maintenance for mountain bikers, not mountain bikes. He is the type of mountain biker that loves to jump off of anything and everything, and is always ready to take a safety break and have a "headset adjustment." With Dangerous there is a different standard of bike maintenance, but come to think of it, that standard may be the norm amongst the Sedona gnarly crew. What that really means is that their bikes never work perfectly, or even close to perfectly, and are a huge frustration for perfectionist mechanics or, for that matter, any normal bicycle mechanic. On the other hand, for mechanics in the know, we know what can be done to those bikes. The rule of thumb is that if there is air in the tires and a few of the gears are working, then the bike is ready to ride, and, no amount of additional "mechanicing" will make things noticeably better for very long.

Dangerous Dave earned his nickname on his first club ride. That may have been the first and only time that someone earned his nickname so fast. Most riders give it a little time before they do something stupid enough to earn their moniker. In Dave's case, he had just crashed off his first jump of the day, and being a chiropractor in training, he thought nothing of having the Bullish Dude adjust him. We knew what the Bullish Dude was capable of, but it didn't seem to faze Dangerous Dave. I guess he was a lot less fragile than he looked, or perhaps the Bullish Dude was just being merciful. Dangerous Dave's trailside maintenance has helped a lot of crashed and tumbled mountain bikers over the years, and it became a standard joke that if he adjusted you on the trail, he didn't charge you. He extended many a mountain bike ride for mountain bikers who thought they were too hurt to continue riding.

I remember the first time Trouble met Dangerous. Trouble had sprained his ankle and was limping towards the road dragging his bike behind him when Dangerous showed up, adjusted his ankle and they both continued on riding. If Dangerous can adjust you within minutes of the injury, that injury heals very quickly and easily and becomes a thing of the past. On another occasion, Simon had literally pulled his shoulder out of its socket on the way to the trail, doing something stupid, of course. Dangerous adjusted his shoulder, got it back in place, and Simon was downhill racing the next day. Maybe not the smartest thing for Simon to do, but has anyone ever said mountain bikers were smart? Gnarly yes! Smart no!

As far as riding-style goes, Dangerous's style is unique among riders and it is probably best to not follow him on a ride, although that could and has been said about most of our riders. Some of which is because you'll either miss a turn and loose the group, as in the case of Amp, or you'll find yourself heading off an obstacle that no one in their right mind would want to do, as in the case of Dangerous and Simon. Dangerous has the uncanny ability of turning a caddywompus approach to an obstacle into a picture perfect jump and landing. Most riders would try the approach again before the launch, but not Danger. He somehow pulls it all together moments before the launch and always lands it without incedent. It might be due to his natural ability, or it could be that I have been teaching him tai chi for the past twenty years, or it could be the continual "headset adjustments," or it could simply be the right combination. I just don't know, and I doubt he does either.

Dave was the classic Sedona mountain biker business owner. For years he would schedule his chiropractic appointments around the club ride schedule and not the client schedule. Nowadays, he is a roving chiropractor with plenty of time to go riding, but in reality his riding time has not increased dramatically. He is mostly consumed with chasing chicks, those infamous "headset adjustments" and being on holiday. Matter of fact, even when Dangerous had his office, I think he was mostly on holiday. He is the only one I know who needs to take a holiday from his holiday.

Another early rider was Skankin Joe. Joe was an old school skateboarder from California. He skated with many of the famous boarders before they became famous. He would tell us stories of the days when someone would be on vacation and the skaters would drain their swimming pools, to be used as a skate park, and then fill them back up before they would return, and no one ever was the wiser. Skanker only rode with us for a short time. We would have to stop by his house on the way to the ride and wake him up. He would then proceed to pound a couple bottles of beer before he could get up and out on his bike. He would also bring along a few bottles of beer for the ride to keep himself going. One time I was riding next to Joe and he hit a sapling tree, which slingshot him backwards. When I caught back up to him wondering if he was okay, he sat up and said, in his cigarette garbled voice, "That was nothing compared to my skateboard days." Joe's greatest feat was pedaling up the Upper Loop road to work at four in the morning. It wasn't uncommon for him to fall asleep, or was that pass out, while riding up the hill to work.

Jules was perhaps the first truly gnarly old dude. He was a fifth-degree black-belt instructor, and each of his three kids was the youngest in turn to earn that title. He once told me that he fought seven days a week for years and never felt as beat up as he did after one of our club rides. He earned the nickname First Blood, not after Stalone, but because he always drew blood on the rides. After the rides he would go down to Lost Avocadoes, I mean Los Abrigados, one of Sedona's fancy spas and get cleaned up, and I earned a nefarious reputation for hurting people from the looks of him with all the blood and scratches. On one Mingus ride, he was ahead of the group and left so much blood on the shrubbery that people were complaining for months.

Gary Appolonairess was another early rider. He was Mexican or Native American; we never knew which. This dude was fit and fast and an incredible rider, and had long black hair and that classic Mayan look. Since he rarely had his own bike, I would put him on the oldest most beat-up bike I could find in an attempt to slow him down. It never worked. Even on a piece of junk bike he was blazingly fast. One year we got ahold of some Russian athlete pills that contained procaine HCl, and I remember he and I would just hammer off the front of the rides. At break time we would stuff our faces with dried fruit and nuts and then we would hammer some more. That may have been my fastest year. Gary earned the name Rocky, after Rocky the Flying Squirrel. There were two incidences on two consecutive rides that sealed his fate. On the first ride, he was going down a steep face of red rock that had a good-sized drop-off at the bottom. When he got to the drop-off, he did an endo, but instead of bailing off the front of the bike like most of us, he somehow stayed with the bike and essentially did a bike somersault while still attached to his pedals. If that wasn't enough, on the next ride we were down by Oak Creek doing a ride that had multiple creek crossings. This was wintertime and the water was very very cold, so cold in fact that after the water crossings, which got our feet wet, it would take thirty seconds of riding with numb feet and excruciating pain and having to visualize that we actually had feet to warm back up. On one of these crossings, I was slowing down to get a good shot at it when Rocky came blazing by me into the water only to have the water stop his bike dead in its tracks. He flew over the handlebars into the water. Since the water was so cold, he literally popped out of the water before it could close over his back. Those two events earned him his nickname.

My favorite nickname story has to do with Jeffrey Roth, more infamously and forever known as the Bogus Dude. I was there and he chose his own name, something that has never been duplicated. This was in the early days of Mountain Bike Heaven, and in those days when the summer doldrums hit Sedona, we would close up shop and go riding. On this particular day, we went up to Williams and had a nice ride on Bill Williams Mountain. On the way back home, we stopped for a movie in Flagstaff. The movie was *Bill & Ted's Bogus Journey*. After the movie, as Jeff was opening his car door, he pointed to himself and uttered the now infamous words Bogus Dude. I pointed back to him in full agreement and repeated those words, Bogus Dude, and the legend was born. To this day, almost twenty years later, he still wears his moniker somewhat reluctantly.

Bogus Dude is unlike anyone else that has ever been lost in Sedona's red rocks. If you look into his eyes, which I don't recommend, you can sense the troubled nature of his soul. He probably isn't dangerous to anyone other than himself, but that in itself might take down the whole of humanity. Actually, I do exaggerate a wee little bit. Humanity doesn't stand a chance. Don't get me wrong; I don't have anything against BD. On the contrary, without him in the world, I might have had to play his role and I doubt I would have been as good at it. It truly amazes me that he has survived on the planet this long, and I am the first to say he has grown and evolved in a more positive way. He is still bogus, he is still angry at the world, but he is a more mature, slightly more responsible Bogus Dude: he has a dog.

It came as no shock to the rest of us when he picked his own nickname. Despite his best efforts to change his name, the nickname has stuck and no doubt will be with him to the bitter end. Some twenty years later, BD doesn't ride a bike much anymore, but the world would be a better and safer place if he did, and most of the bike riders still know him as the Bogus Dude. If he had been born in a different era, for example before the wheel was invented, he would have made the wheel square, a little more bounce a little more resistance and a lot more bogus. One season, many years ago, Bogus lived in the woods and dug himself a huge hole to live in, which was dubbed the Bogus Hole. To this day, neither he nor I can locate the said hole, but I did recently run into an old Sedona friend who did stumble upon the Bogus Hole years ago when he was old hiking about. At first he was a bit confused as to what it was, but then remembered the stories and the light bulb went off. He brought this story to my attention recently when we were reminiscing about the good old days and it brought a huge belly laugh to both of us.

ADVENTURE RIDES

Those were some of the earliest riders who helped define the Sedona mountain bike community, but the riders kept coming and the bikes kept breaking and the nicknames kept being doled out. By then we had discovered all sorts of trails that mountain bikes could ride on. Some were legal trails while others were in designated wilderness, which was illegal for mountain bikes to be in, but legal for cows and mining. That never seemed to stop us in the early days, after all, bikes did far less damage to the trails than cows, and when it came to forest circus politics, mountain bikers tended to disagree with pretty nearly everyone. Our two favorite early wilderness adventure rides were Brins Mesa and Jacks Canyon. Both of these trails are on the extreme end of the spectrum of what a mountain biker can ride, especially using the early technology. They would become favorite trails for extreme mountain bikers for years to come, and the fact that they were illegal made them that much more fun. Kind of like the forbidden fruit. These trails are so extreme that they are still a challenge to mountain bikers today in the age of super fat tires and long travel suspension. Not that we ever ride in designated wilderness these days.

Another extreme place to ride is Mingus Mountain, above Cottonwood and Jerome. The first adventures on Mingus were screaming downhill descents on dirt roads where flat tires ruled the day. I think six flats was the record, but on at least one occasion, I was the only rider to survive the ride with air in my tires. That ride Crazy Steve spent an hour stuffing pine needles into his tire to try and ride out, only to have those needles pulverize into dust within seconds, and Bogus Dude ended up tying a bandanna around his tire to hold it in place. On one Mingus ride we were determined to find a single track descent, so we unwittingly followed an old mining or lumber road down until it dead ended. Instead of doing the smart thing, which would have been backtracking, we set out bushwhacking off the side of Mingus Mountain without having any clue as to where we were going. We had to throw our bikes over huge manzanitas and then scurry underneath them. Somehow, against all odds and common sense, we found the Coleman trail and the Mingus ride took on a whole new light. There was a picture from that day of the gnarly crew sitting under a large shade tree with blood streaks dripping down all of our legs. We thought that once we found a single track down, it would be the end of the blood, but we were wrong. The shrubbery was so dense on the Coleman trail that we would often resort to sending the Bullish Dude in front to open up a path for the rest of us. On one occasion, we had a very petite girl named Ivy along who simply did not have enough body mass to bash her way through. When Cosmic Ray included this ride in his guidebook, *Fat Tire Tales and Trails*, an unsuspecting group of out-of-towners ventured down the trail and sent him their new name for the trail, "Revenge of the Vegetables."

There has been at least one near-death experience on the Mingus ride. It is a great ride and includes switchbacks, drop-offs, dense shrubbery, cactus, and exposure—all the necessary components for a great adventure. It only has one place where the exposure is so extreme that it could cause death, and you guessed it, that was the place where Simon taught us, and himself, that mountain bikes and mountain bikers can fly. Simon's near-death experience just happened to occur when we had a journalist along, and the story with a picture did appear in a mountain bike magazine years ago. As I've often said, there is something about being on a stage that brings out the best; I mean, the worst out of mountain bikers. That day Simon and Wheelie were racing down the Black Canyon trail at breakneck speed. Simon was not used to having anyone that close to him on a descent, and that day Wheelie was right on his tail. Simon hit a rock on that exposed stretch and his bike flew off a 100-foot cliff; okay, it may have been only ninety-nine feet. In all logic, Simon should have gone along with the bike, but his angels thought otherwise and somehow some way he didn't. What he did do was contort his body in some strange way and found himself grasping some wimpy shrub on the edge of the cliff. To this day, Simon has no clue how he did this, because the bush that he ended up grabbing was nowhere near where he was heading off. I guess it just wasn't his time.

On another Mingus ride, we unexpectedly ran into knee-deep snow. We had a heck of a time staying on the trail that day and kept on loosing it and having to backtrack to find it again. We only were able to ride when we got below the snow line. One participant commented that he had a great time on the snowy hike-a-bike, but the last hour of riding was way over his head.

Another area to ride, which is often forgotten, is the Turkey Creek/House Mountain/Verde Valley School area. House Mountain is one of the hardest, steepest, longest climbs in Sedona. It's not used too often, because once on top there aren't a lot of options of where to go. Usually, once on top, the easiest choice is to turn around and head back down the trail. Of course, a rest at the top is in order first. One day we scoped out a way to cruise over the top and down one of the other sides. On this first—and perhaps only—attempt at this particular route, Simon ended up by twisting his ankle, and when he got to a place that had a huge drop-off, too big to ride, he handed me his bike to help get it down. I did the only thing that seemed logical to do with Simon's bike, and that was to throw it off the cliff. Well, what else was a guy to do; it was Simon's bike and was used to launching drops. I had already thrown my bike down the drop and it wasn't used to that kind of abuse, but they both survived.

Over the years, we found several other routes off of House Mountain. The four-hour wash, which has sizable drop-offs and isn't used very often, and, the more infamous and more often used three-hour wash. The three-hour wash has become a standard of what a gnarly ride is, and let me tell you, it is not for the faint of heart, although there was one gal who enjoyed walking her bike down this wash because it was such a cool place to be. On a good day, I might ride seventy to seventy-five percent of the wash, but Dangerous Dave would ride upwards of ninety-five percent. We would watch him perform feats in that wash that defied reason, logic, and bike abuse.

The adventures kept going and the riders kept showing up for our club rides and Sedona was earning its reputation as a premier mountain bike destination. Moab and Durango had come first, but Sedona had much better trail access, and as the trail system grew, it became clear that we had more closer-in technical single track than anywhere else on the planet.

One day, our first mountain bike celebrity came down from Flagstaff to ride with us. Joe Murray, arguably the most accomplished mountain bike racer of all time, showed up and taught us one of his secrets. Joe didn't ride with a little or inner chainring on his bike. That meant he always pushed bigger gears and therefore went faster. We tried it, and sure enough we went faster, but the problem for us was, we didn't have the level of fitness or the strength that Joe had, and would have to resort back to the little chainring to catch our breath. For those of you who don't know about Joe Murray's accomplishments, he won twelve straight NORBA mountain bike races in 1985, and in a career of racing in 233 events, he won seventy-three times. There was a rumor, years ago, that he won many of those races while on a mind-altering substance. When I asked him about it one day, he simply smiled and denied the allegations, but his denial never really convinced me. I guess that is one rumor that may never be laid to rest. For a celebrity, Joe is a great and humble guy, and to this day is still blazingly fast. He was also one of the early frame designers who is credited with developing the radically sloping top tube, which gives much more frame stand over height clearance. We still run into Joe out on Sedona's trails, especially in the winter after Flagstaff is snowed in.

As the years went by, we joined up with some of the Flagstaff mutants and would ride up there especially on hot summer days. My two favorite Flagstaff guides were Long Tall and the infamous Dan Diaz. Both of these riders were exceptional, and since in those days Flag was a technology-challenged zone, they both rode double-rigid bikes. We rode many trails that even today are almost impossible to ride. I remember Long Tall taking us on the now famous Blue Dot trail more than a decade before it became a popular thing to do. He warned us that there was a dude with a turban who didn't like mountain bikers on the trail and would put branches on the trail in an attempt to block its use. Years later, when the trail became popular, the newbies became irate about this dude always blocking the trail. I would scratch my head and look at them and say, "Well, it's not a new thing." That guy has been blocking the trail for over a decade". They were thinking the trail was a recent discovery, but that was just not the way it was, and all old timers knew what to expect. Kids, they think they know and own everything!

Dan Diaz, our other Flagstaff trail guide, took us on the old trails when they had old names. I remember Fossil Ridge shortly after it was burned and how now it has a new name and people think it's a new trial. I miss those days when our Flagstaff trail guides knew the original names of the trails. The other thing I miss about the early Flag rides was that we never ever drove to the trailhead—that was sacrilege. We always left from someone's house in town and got to ride various combinations of the urban trail system. Oh, well, I guess we have gotten softer and lazier in our old age. I still try and convince people that we should ride those urban trails, but most times it only falls on deaf ears. With all the new development, it's harder to find a way to the trials—NOT! The other great thing about Flag is the Black Bean after a good long dusty day of riding.

The best story from Flagstaff is yet to come: The day The NOD showed us all what he was made of, as if we didn't know. We were doing our favorite loop around Mount Elden. This is a longish ride with lots of cool trail connections. It's a six-hour loop if we do the short version, and the group can get stretched out. On this particular day, Dangerous, The Nod, and I had gone off the front. We had finished with the techy Hobbit Enchanted Forest part of the ride, which is very slow and methodical, and we had finally gotten to a place where we could hammer and stretch out our legs, and that's what we were doing. We were just turning up on a trail when we ran into a skinny older man with a staff. He reminded me of someone out of *Lord of the Rings*. He uttered the now infamous words at us, "You guys don't belong here." The instant those words were out of his mouth, I knew that trouble would ensue. You just don't say those words when The NOD is around. That is always a recipe for conflict. One time a horse rider said those words to The NOD, and he almost punched the horse out. On this particular day, I responded logically with a simple question about whether the trail was in designated wilderness. To me, that is the only type of trail that mountain bikers don't belong on. Old Man Elden responded in the negative, and I scooted around him before he could react and was gone. Next up was Dangerous Dave. Danger tried to follow me but was unsuccessful due to the Old Man grabbing his bike and blocking his way. Danger and Old Man Elden got into a tussle with Danger, his bike and the Old Man rolling down the hill, with Danger saying, "Dude, I don't want to hurt you; I'm a doctor." Eventually, Danger climbed back up the hill with his bike, got on his bike, and was off. Now it was

The NOD's turn and his response will live on in infamy. The Old Man blocked NOD's passage and without so much as a word, The NOD unleashed a powerful left hook and decked the obstructer. After that, Old Man Elden uttered, "Can we talk about this?" The NOD's response was, "We already have!" At that time, the hoots from the rest of the group were heard, which meant more riders, some of which can be quite aggressive. In a flash of an eye, Old Man Elden was gone and that was a good thing, because as I said, some of the other riders might have really hurt that dude. To this day, I don't know why Old Man Elden thought we didn't belong, but when I told the story to Long Tall, he said, "All you guys really needed to do was to take away his staff." I guess, the lesson to be learned is that when you encounter on old man on the trail with a staff, watch out. There is something about a staff or a stick that empowers these old dudes.

On another occasion, we encountered a belligerent old man with a stick. This time we were on a local Sedona trail, and again I was in the lead and hammering. In order not to interfere with the old hiker dude plodding along, I took one of the many shortcuts on that trail and was able to pass the guy by without getting in his way. For some reason, he took offense to that and uttered something unintelligible at me. Most likely an obscenity, but I was gone before his words caught up to me. Further behind me was a gal named Eden; she followed my shortcut and since, by then, the hiker was closer to the shortcut, his words were intelligible to Eden, who responded in like fashion and asked the old guy whether he wanted his stick stuck up his butt. Well, that goes to show that like energy yields a like response. I was sure that we would hear about that incident through a complaint to the forest circus, but luck was on our side, or perhaps the old guy was embarrassed that a girl would respond to him that way, who knows. I guess sometimes people feel that a trail only has one route and to use an obvious shortcut is not acceptable. I personally feel that a shortcut is a great way to get around a slow biker or hiker without causing any problems. But that may be just me.

One of the greatest adventure rides of all time is Casner Mooney. Of course, the Mooney part of this ride is designated wilderness, but I can't go along with not using an old cattle trail that the cows chew up so bad that no one else can use it, except for extreme mountain bikers. The first time we tried to do this route, we were turned back by lighting strikes right above our heads. It was the day that Crazy Steve showed us he was truly a poet by writing about the "once gnarly crew." I can't remember the exact poem, but I do remember that I was very impressed with Crazy's poetic genius. That day we had completed the legal part of the ride, the hour-plus-long, hike-a-bike part that brought us to the top of the Casner Mountain climb. The weather was not in our favor, and at the top we encountered severe lightning strikes above our head on the electric wires that were overhead. We had no idea how far the rest of the trail was, so we chickened out and headed back down the Casner Mountain trail before we encountered the rain that usually comes along with lightning. I think on that day the rain may not have come, and that was what inspired Crazy Steve to write his epic poem. The Mooney part was left for another day.

I do remember a few of the incidents that occurred on various adventures up there. There was the time that Bogus

Dude rode his bike over Roxanne's helmet at the top of the climb. That day we did the ride as a full moon extravaganza and the moon was green as it set. On another occasion, as we were heading out of the lower part of the trail, we encountered a bull. Rocky and I were way off the front of the ride and we chased that bull for quite a while until it yielded the trail. But one of the last riders of that day wasn't as lucky. I guess that bulls can be quite fierce when their minds are set, and after a bunch of riders had passed him by, he was ready to hold his ground. Jules First Blood seemed to attract his full angst. He was the last rider to pull out that day and had to give the bull a very wide berth, which meant he veered way off the trail to get around that bull. I'm a bit surprised they didn't have a showdown, but even a fifth-degree black belter knows when to yield. I was quite impressed.

The Casner Mooney ride was what I chose for my fortieth birthday ride. We once again did it as a full-moon ride. That day I rode more of the uphill than I ever did before. I am a notorious climber and I had set up my bike's gears for climbing that day. So I pedaled my way up while Bullish dude set out hike-a-biking. These super extreme climbs are hell on drive trains, and Bullish knew from past experiences that his drive train would not have held up on the climb if he had pedaled. It took me a full three quarters of the ride to catch up to the Bullish Dude, and we reached the top almost at the same time. As the years went on, most of us have resorted to the Bullish method just because. That day the rest of the ride went off without any major catastrophes and we had a great ride finishing up before eight in the morning. But that was only the first part of the birthday celebration. Later that day, we headed down to Phoenix by car to catch a great Bob Dylan and Paul Simon concert. The odd thing was that on our way down to Phoenix, we were passed by this ratty-looking pickup truck that was heading down from Flagstaff. Lo and behold, sleeping in the bed of that truck was the Bullish Dude. That was one birthday that I will always remember. Birthday rides are usually special adventures, and in the old days, they generally were super gnarly adventure rides.

The NOD's fifty-fifth birthday was another one of those great adventures. In those days, The NOD was our senior role model. There may have been other Nods that rode with us, but The NOD was definitely a step ahead of all of them as far as gnarlyness goes. That day he chose the Yankee Doodle trail in Prescott. I can't remember if that was our first time, but more likely it was our second shot at it. There was a Prescott gal named Deb, who was our local trail guide. Trust me when I say there was no other gal in Sedona or Prescott that would act in this capacity for this ride. Most people don't even know or want to know that this trail exists. I had recently purchased a small first generation JVC digital video camera and played with it on the ride. Sadly, that video was lost somewhere over the years. I do remember that we found an old 1940s rusted-out car on the trail and we got The NOD to sit in it for pictures. I also remember him saying the word "fifty-five" while he was sitting in that old car. As you might have guessed, Yankee Doodle is not your average run-of-the-mill mountain bike trail. It is a rutted-out cattle trail that descends into a valley on the other side of Prescott, away from everything. It has a nasty climb at the beginning before you get to the radical descent. The first climb is nothing compared with the climb out of that valley on the back side. This ride is not for the faint of heart, but it was very fitting for The NOD's fifty-fifth birthday adventure.

With our local trail guide along, we were able to do the ride the correct way with a huge single track hike-a-bike in the middle. On subsequent attempts, we missed that single track and ended up having to do an obscenely long double track climb that just wasn't as much fun. We may be the only mountain bike crew that considers an hour-long hike-a-bike the preferred route to a rideable climb. But that just shows what kind of riders we are. I guess there is something infinitely more satisfying about pulling off a super gnarly adventure, or perhaps we are just crazy. That day we ended up taking along an unsuspecting out-of-towner who did admirably well. His only incident was a flat tire, which he actually rolled off the rim so completely that the tire turned completely inside out. With green slime everywhere and an inside-out tire, it looked like something out of an alien invasion.

One time we did the Yankee Doodle ride with burro bikes. The NOD, Simon, and I had gotten these small-wheeled, fat-tire bikes that were designed for backcountry trekking. The NOD's and mine had front shocks on them, but Simon's was double-rigid. Simon being the crazy downhiller that he was, pushed that bike and himself to the limits. He and Chewy, one of the shop mechanics, raced downhill through all the loose rocks and ruts, and despite his best efforts, Chewy could not drop Simon. Chewy was riding a regular double-suspended, twenty-six-inch-wheeled bike, and Simon was on the twenty-inch-wheeled, double rigid burro bike. Who would have thought that Simon could keep up? That day, we got lost, riding an extra hour on a great single track in the wrong direction and climbing for miles out of the way. We were lucky that our local trail guide that day, a super buff mostly road rider named Toby, finally figured out that we were heading out and not back or we might have found ourselves in Phoenix. That was the day we ended up climbing the double track back. Simon paid the price for his extremely fast descent on the small-wheeled bike by having to climb out with a splitting headache. I figured he had simply shaken his brain loose.

Another heinous hike-a-bike ride, and I do mean heinous is the Seven Springs adventure. This one is north of Phoenix, and requires logistics and a long car drive, neither of which is a skill that most mountain bikers possess. It also requires seasonal timing. It must be done in the winter, to avoid the extreme heat of Phoenix, and has to be done when the river is not too high to cross. This is a seven-hour ride if nothing goes wrong and includes at least an hour and a half of hike-a-biking. The ride is one of those that while your doing it, you keep wondering why, and keep saying, "I will never do this again." But once completed there is such a high level of satisfaction of accomplishment that you immediately begin planning for the next time. On the first attempt, we didn't know there was a loop and ended up in Cave Creek via some old dirt roads. This meant that we had twenty miles of paved and dirt roads to pedal to get back to our vehicles. So, after a huge meal at some Mexican restaurant, DR and I volunteered to pedal back to the vehicles and then pick up the rest of the riders in town. It seemed to take forever, but as we learned on later adventures, it was a much less ambitious way of doing the ride.

On another occasion, we took along a rider who was not really prepared for the brutality of the loop. His fitness level just was not up to the length and brutality of the ride and he slowed the entire group down to the point that we had to finish in the dark. We almost lost Georgeus George that day, but a few riders hung back with him as it got dark while the others, who had already gotten back, found flashlights and lit the way to the finish. We never made that mistake again, always starting ultra early in the morning and making sure that everyone was aware of what they were getting into. The most distinguishing feature of the Seven Springs area are the huge saguaro cactuses there. These suckers are so king-sized and are in such good shape, not like the ones in the center of the highway that either get shot up or look half dead from the car emissions, that their memory will always be etched in my mind. I still consider doing this ride every year even though I know better. It has been several years since I've done it, but after writing about the adventure, I am planning to do it as soon as possible.

There is one other hike-a-bike ride that we haven't done for years that comes to mind. It was our St. Patty's Day special adventure when St. Patty's Day was a huge Sedona event. In the old days, the St. Patty's Day Parade was Sedona's biggest party. Route 89A would get closed off from Dry Creek Road to Soldier's Pass, and everyone would come out for the parade. We would watch it from the roof of Mountain Bike Heaven and have the best seats in the house. The best part, from our standpoint, was the after-parade drinking parties. After the parade, a huge number of people would head into the forest for picnics and green beer. This occupied the forest circus, and we would head up to Sterling Pass for a huge hike-a-bike. I can't even remember how long it would take us to top out, but I do remember the great descent into Vaultee Arch. The forest was so deadening to our noise that it reminded me of a Monty Python-type soundtrack as the herd of mountain bikers did their best to ride impossible switchbacks and crazy downhill obstacles. If you can imagine moans and groans and *wahoos* falling on a contained dense forest insulation, that was what it was like.

Of course, there was also the prospect of flying mountain bikers. This was always a very special ride, being one of those wilderness extravaganzas. To add icing to the cake, we would pull out on Vaultee Arch Road and then once again get our added thrills by going over Brins Mesa, making it a double wilderness ride. There was never a chance of getting caught by the forest circus because they had their hands full breaking up drunken St. Patty's Day brawls in the woods. Of course, we never caused any real damage as wilderness designations in Sedona are purely a political thing and has nothing to do with resource damage, just control. Furthermore, when these trails were originally created, they were created for use without stipulation as to who could use them, making them a personal property right, and it doesn't matter what government agency later would oversee them. The right-of-way was established first and trumps the government regulators every time.

One year we actually got the okay to have a mountain bike race. It was part of a Heart Association race that included a running event as well as a mountain bike race. I was convinced we wouldn't get the go-ahead, but Big

Trouble was the liaison with the forest circus and he had his mind set and would not take no as an answer. It turned out that the addition of the mountain bike race was what allowed the event to be profitable. To this day, that was the only mountain bike race that the forest circus has ever sanctioned and allowed. We used the first part of the Deadman's Pass trail and the old cycle cross race course and put together a six-mile loop that was fun and challenging. It was a challenge to find a route that was on the system, and I made Bill Stafford, from the forest circus, actually hike in the woods for seven hours. The beginners did one lap, the sport racers did two laps, and we made the expert racers do four laps. There were a few injuries and lots of entertainment and no one complained. The expert winner of the race was a Flagstaff mountain man with a huge beard, who passed our local favorite, Wheelie, on the fourth lap while singing a song. Those Flagstaff mountain men live in the woods even in the winter and are generally tougher than tough. I must say that when we had the review with the forest circus after the event, it started out being a Rag-O-Rama session until I got to speak up. At that point, I got to set things straight, especially with the forest circus law enforcement officer, who pretty nearly took out the lead rider by opening his truck door into him. By the end of that meeting, the energy had shifted from an event that had many problems to an event that had few problems. I just wished that the forest circus personnel paid more attention to their job instead of bitching and moaning about long-standing problems that all the trail users knew were not related to or caused by our event. Maybe one of these days the forest circus will agree to sanction another Sedona mountain bike race.

One of my fondest memories of that race was when Mattster, a sport racer, coasted into the staging area with a broken chain and a lit joint hanging out of his mouth. He was thinking that his race was over since he was not able to repair his chain on his own. Instead, I fixed his chain for him and he was on his way in no time ready to finish his next lap. By the way, he still had that lit joint in his mouth as he pedaled away. Another memory I have from that race is of Bike Daddy Chad, one of our mechanics, on the roof of the bike shop directing people to the staging area in his slow motion, tai chi-type way.

MOUNTAIN BIKE HEAVEN
THE PROGRESSION

How it came to pass that I opened Mountain Bike Heaven in the first place is a story in itself. One person, Scott Barry, later to earn the nickname Snake, may have been the most impressed. He had met me through Jeffrey Bogus Dude, and that may have biased him to begin with. But, when I did open the shop, he was one of my earliest supporters along with Simon.

In those days, the bike shop was in a 500-square-foot building, and I slept in the back, not being able to afford a real place to live. It was so cramped in those days that I had to jam the bikes in, in such a way that the front door would barely close. I was able to put bikes out in front of the shop, and there was only one way they came out. The bike shop was so cramped that I could only have one or maybe two people in there at a time. I may have stayed there forever, except my friend Dianna worked in the flower shop down the street. The owners of the flower shop were building their own building, and Dianna and Joe, the landlord, decided that my bike shop would move in once the flower shop moved out. This was all decided long before I was ever notified of their decision. When I was informed, it seemed like the perfect place. I moved the shop in three days, being open in both locations and not missing a beat. That was kind of funny, considering that another bike shop was trying to open at the same time and had recently postponed their opening for another month. I guess some people are perfectionists and others just want to have fun and help people.

I had one overriding principle in those days, and that was to provide a place for people to get in touch with the child within. Of all the things that I have accomplished with Mountain Bike Heaven, that is the one that gave me the most satisfaction. When someone takes a test ride and comes back with a huge shit-eating grin on their face, I know that they have touched that inner child. If you can remember that far back, the first bike represents freedom, freedom to go where you want when you want to, and freedom of movement. That freedom is why it's very hard, if not impossible, to control mountain bikers. They want to be able to go anywhere and everywhere without having anyone telling them they can't go here or they can't go there. I feel that mountain bikers have gotten a bad rap over the years because they are always out there having way more fun than other user groups.

There has been a huge progression of mechanics over the years at Mountain Bike Heaven. The first generation of mechanics was Bogus Dude, Crazy Steve, and me. Then there was Tal, a Celtic gay dude who wasn't much of a bike rider or a mechanic for that matter, but he was very good with the customers and sold a lot of bikes. Things began to class up when Wheelie showed up. Wheelie Todd showed up riding a taxicab yellow Continental- logoed Steelman hand-built frame with a pot leaf as the emblem on the head tube. He was a great mechanic, good with most customers, and an incredible bike rider. He had bike-handling skills beyond most people's wildest dreams. One of his earliest feats was to jump off the back shed onto the flat ground. That shed was at least ten feet tall. Some people might consider that kind of jump to be bike abuse, but not Wheelie.

He was a New York boy, and had honed his skills jumping off loading docks in the city. He was also an early BMXer, and when we had our mountain bike race team, he won a State Expert Championship in the most competitive age group.

As we moved into the bigger location, business boomed, and sales doubled overnight. We could now get more than one person in the shop at a time and needed another mechanic on staff. Enter in, Ezra Rubik, another New Yorker. Ez was a sous chef who my friend Chef Todd introduced to me. He was also a determined bike rider and racer, earning the nickname the Chicken Hawk when he raced, and he also won an Expert State Championship. It was a good thing that Ezra and Wheelie raced in different age groups. Ezra would listen to very loud, dark, devil worship music in the shop, which didn't always go over that well with our customers.

Next up was Shop George. George was not a racer, but was a great mechanic, having a long history of bike-shop experience from Illinois to Tempe. He had a Chicago-type demeanor, which rubbed certain customers the wrong way until they got to know him. Even in a bike shop, you can't please all the people all the time, and if someone was overly arrogant, I would make no bones out of kicking them out. George married a mountain bike gal named Laura, and Mountain Bike Heaven had its first and only female employee. She and Geo ran the shop together for a while, but I'm not sure that having a couple working together is always a good thing. When they took a holiday, I would always be doubly shorthanded.

One year I had a roommate who couldn't pay rent consistently, so I had to put him to work if I wanted to be able to pay my rent. Most times we would have a mechanic and a front-counter person. Everyone had to be able to fix flat tires, since Sedona is the home of flat tires. One of my standard jokes is that everywhere else they have fat tire festivals, but in Sedona, we have flat tire festivals.

The years went on, and the mechanics and front people kept evolving; after all, this was Sedona, and everyone evolves in Sedona. One year we had Tim in the bike shop. He was a good mechanic and a good rider as well. His bike shop dharma jaded him so much that he became a jeweler.

Then we had the Chewy, Dean, Dave, NOD, and Shaggy years. Egos in the mountain bike mechanic world, just like in real life, get in the way of working together effectively. It did in the past and it really got bad during this phase. This group may have been both the best of life at Mountain Bike Heaven and the worst of life. The NOD was the front man, mostly taking care of customers and creating more logos for Mountain Bike Heaven than any bike shop deserved to have. The Dean, Dave, and Chewy trio were perhaps the best mechanics in Sedona, but as far as working together, they sucked. They were always ragging on each other, and this got in the way of productivity and customer service. They would spend time talking amongst themselves and ignore the customers. Or, in Dean's case, he would spend his time trying to pickup chicks and give super overly detailed trail info. Don't get me wrong, they were all great guys, and could be great mechanics as well, when they wanted to be. The biggest problem was that they each really wanted to do the other's job, because in their mind, that was the easy job.

Eventually, the economy started to tank, and by the way, that was years before they officially declared it a recession, and cutbacks had to occur. That was definitely the hardest thing that I have ever had to do in the twenty-plus years that I had owned Mountain Bike Heaven. It was clear that business was heading down, and I had a huge rent payment at that time. So one year, I had to let Dean and Dave go. Chewy had already departed for another bike shop where he could get more hours. That left Rob Gnarly, NOD, myself, Shaggy on Wednesdays so I could do the club ride, and George on the weekends.

Rob Gnarly had shown up from Telluride a few years back and had hung out at the bike shop until there was an opening for him. He started out filling Chewy's spot and, after the big cutback when I had to let Dean and Dave go, became the main mechanic, along with George and me. His forte was working with the kids, and at that point in time, the kids were where our money was coming from. Kids are the future of the planet, and Rob had his hand on that pulse. His downfall was that he loved the kids so much, he would let them chew up all his time and left more and more of the mechanicing to me. That sucked from my perspective. After being in business nearly twenty years, here I was working on junk bike repairs again. It was becoming clear to me that my time in the mountain bike business was coming to an end.

I guess I knew that the writing was on the wall several years before I was finally able to pull the plug. Sedona was no longer a real-estate mecca; matter of fact, the real estate market had been our lifeblood, just like every other business in town. Sure, tourism was still strong and perhaps even growing, but I had always viewed that as the icing on the cake, and as we all know, icing is not very nourishing even if it tastes good. We had always relied upon new people moving into town after buying their new house, and then needing a new bike or having to update an old one. That market had literally stopped and with the addition of more bike shops in town, we were all left with trying to cut up the icing.

One day a year or two before I closed, I had a tai chi student of mine ask me why I continued to do the bike shop. He had been around long enough to see my struggle and even if I wasn't ready to let go, he knew that I should. My initial response was very defensive, mostly saying that I was there to allow mountain bikers a way to ride and make a living at the same time. Notice that I didn't say, or for that matter feel, anything about helping people find that child within. I had literally lost touch with my guiding principle. The business had taken over and as the economy continued to tank, I just couldn't continue to subsidize it anymore. I could no longer help people with their bikes just to help them; my resources had been eaten up and I was left with only my heart. That night, I kept hearing that young man's words in my ears: "why do you continue with this?" When I awoke the next morning, I realized that it was okay to let go of this project. I didn't need a legacy and I certainly could do something else. That young tai chi student was my greatest teacher and I felt so much lighter and was ready to move on.

To many people, it may have appeared that I had moved on years ago, but the burdens of business are not always obvious. It took me several more years to actually figure out how to extradite myself from Mountain Bike Heaven, making a futile attempt to sell or even pass on my dream, but that was not to come to pass. Since I like milestones, I chose to close the shop up on my fifty-fifth birthday. I had one goal left with respect to the business, and that was to make sure that Joe, my landlord and good friend for the last fifteen years, would be able to rent the location. That was accomplished when another bike shop business grabbed the spot. I gave them the traditional Sedona welcome by making them feel that they had wronged me by not providing any respect or compensation to me for the nearly twenty years of having a bike business in that location and for being the driving influence in turning Sedona into the mountain bike mecca that it is today. But in reality, they represented what I had spent the last twenty years fighting against, becoming another yuppie bike shop. The truth was that I really didn't care, because I was free, and I knew that the universe would always provide for me, and that Sedona is a place for karma.

So here I was on my fifty-fifth birthday and I closed the bike shop, not really knowing what my next step would be, except that this book was ready to come out. By the way, for the last five days of Mountain Bike Heaven, I was in a seminar actually writing the first draft of this book. It kept me busy while the reality of what I was about to do sunk in. I began Mountain Bike Heaven just after my first Saturn return and closed her down just prior to my second Saturn return. How more auspicious can you get! In truth, I am amazed I was able to stay in business that long. It was never part of my plan to be here in Sedona for nearly twenty-five years. My favorite way of telling people about my business plan is by saying, "I opened with a five-year plan, and twenty years later I made a second five-year plan." That second plan was to get out of dodge.

As I think back on all those rides and riders and bikes and repairs and flat tires, I realize that I accomplished everything I set out to do. I really did something much greater than just fix more flat tires than anyone deserves to have to do in a hundred lifetimes. I was a huge part of turning Sedona into the greatest mountain bike destination on the planet. Don't get me wrong; I didn't do it single-handedly. I had a lot of help! I became the ringleader for one of the greatest mountain bike families ever created. I simply was in the right place at the right time with the right vision. This book is my thank you to that family, all who came and saw and played. I wish you luck at all your endeavors and hope you never lose sight of that child within and that quest for freedom. Thank you, all of you. And you can bet your last dollar that it is better to live your visions and create your dreams than to not dream at all. I did, and I still have a smile on my face and I know that I am ready to create a new dream, and I can feel it bubbling up from within as I reach completion of my old dream.

THE SEDONA 5

The greatest mountain bike adventure of all times was our ride in the Grand Canyon and the resultant helicopter ride out at sunset. It may not have been the gnarliest bike ride, but it sure was the most publicized and spectacular. We were written up in mountain bike magazines, local newspapers, and best of all, the *Phoenix New Times*. That article in The New Times received the prestigious Arizona Press Club's Sports Article of the Year, something that *New Times* had never won before or since.

The adventure began when the Republicans closed the government down over budgetary bickering. In those days, that was a unique experience, not like nowadays where the threat of closure seems like a daily occurrence. Well, that time it was unique, and Mitch, the Wheeze, took the opportunity to get a group of us together to ride the Grand Canyon. Mitch had wanted to ride the Canyon since he was a kid, and this seemed like the perfect opportunity. So, five of us were drawn together for this purpose. There was Dangerous Dave, Forest, Long Tall, Mitch the Wheeze, and myself. We needed two cars for this adventure, one at the North Rim where we would start the ride, and the other at the South Rim, which would be our shuttle vehicle once we completed the ride. Not knowing how long the government would be closed made the adventure a bit more pressing. Four of us were from Sedona and we got ourselves prepared and organized without incident. It wasn't until we got to Flag to pickup Long Tall that the adventure really got interesting. It was already eleven in the evening when we got to Flagstaff, and Long Tall had lent out his bike, and was in the process of trying to locate it. He knew the general area of where his bike was; it's just that he didn't know exactly where the bike was. It took over an hour of searching around and knocking on doors at midnight for Long Tall to stumble upon where his bike was, and then we were off on the adventure of a lifetime.

We dropped Dangerous Dave's old Monte Carlo at the South Rim, and then loaded everything into my Toyota 4Runner and headed for the North Rim. Let me tell you that it is a long ass drive to the North Rim, but our timing was perfect and we got there just before sunrise. We were on our bikes in no time, all layered up to deal with the cold morning start. It was a short ride to the North Rim trail, and when we entered the Canyon, the sun was up and beginning to warm us up, and the layers started coming off.

The trail was a series of switchbacks and large water bars. It wasn't the most technical of rides we had ever done, but it certainly was the most spectacular one. The steep walls of the Canyon and the incredible views were a sight to behold, and as the day wore on, we warmed up and got into the rhythm of the ride.

At the bridge over the Colorado River, our first riders made a lot of noise, which ultimately led to the downfall of our adventure. One of the homeowners radioed ahead to the authorities that there were bikes in the Canyon, which was a big no-no. By the time we reached Phantom Ranch, the rangers were waiting to apprehend us. We were caught. If there had been a real emergency in the Canyon that day, the rangers would have been caught with their pants down, so to speak, because they had all their troops trying to make bikes in the Canyon into a serious crime. They had us sitting on a volleyball court for what seemed like hours while they checked our IDs to make sure we weren't escaped cons or wanted for having too much fun or something like that. Then the fun really began: the helicopter ride out at sunset. We couldn't understand why they didn't make us hike-a-bike out, which was our original plan, but you know the government; they wanted to spend as much money as possible to show how much power they had and to reinforce why the government was closed in the first place. They handcuffed us and shackled us and then loaded us two at a time into the helicopter and took us up to the holding cell on the South Rim. The enforcers tried to scare us with a story about if we moved quickly they would shoot us, but we were in awe of the sights to behold, a sunset flight out of the Grand Canyon. Later we found out how special that ride really was, you literally cannot buy such a ride at any price. They had kept us on the ground for so long that by the third trip with the helicopter, they were not allowed to touch down, and Dangerous Dave had to climb a ladder to get in. He did have his leg shackles removed for that. As we waited in the holding cell, the National Park Enforcement Rangers were trying to figure out what to do with us. They finally decided to release us, even though we didn't have enough money for bail, mostly because none of them really wanted to drive us to Flagstaff.

Our court date was a few weeks off, and during that time, Mitch created the Sedona 5 website. On the website, he had a poll that showed over seventy percent positive reaction to our adventure. The next part of our ordeal was court. We spent the morning talking with the court clerk, or at least an hour and a half. During that time, we had him rolling with laughter, as we helped him solve all the Canyon's problems. We realized that from his perspective what we had done was minor. He finally had to kick us up to the judge, saying he had forty-seven more cases to process that day. The judge was another story. He knew we didn't take him very seriously, so he started out on a tirade about us being the stupidest people ever to be in his court. I guess he figured that if we weren't going to take him seriously, he was sure going to make sure that we wouldn't respect him either. Well, it worked. I'm sure that stupidity is a crime in the Grand Canyon, and that judges regularly have to prosecute stupidity as a federal crime. But this judge was going to say what he wanted regardless of whether it pertained to laws or crimes or anything. He harangued us for a while, said he doubted that we had learned our lesson when we said we had, and was just about to put us on supervised probation until he found out we had paid our fines. When he realized we had paid our fines, he changed it to unsupervised probation. As an afterthought, as we were about to leave the court, the judge asked the arresting rangers whether there was any resource damage. It was clear from their blank stares as they looked at each other that they hadn't checked and didn't really care. The result was that we lost our bikes and had to pay $244.00 for that spectacular helicopter ride out at sunset that you can't buy commercially at any price.

For us, that was only the beginning. We were an overnight sensation mostly because of the Internet. Sedona got publicity, and IMBA came to town, and our forest circus actually sponsored an IMBA trail ride, and for the first time, several forest circus employees were paid to ride mountain bikes. I guess they were afraid that Sedona might become an area for belligerent mountain bikers. Oh, I forgot, it already was. The official mountain bike community boohooed us, calling us juvenile delinquents or some such silliness, but the real mountain bikers loved us. I even remember having a seventy-year-old guy come into Mountain Bike Heaven and shake my hand for riding my bike in the Grand Canyon. As you may know, when in business, publicity is a bonus whether good or bad. The Sedona 5 was on everyone's lips for a few months until we were forgotten. Periodically, someone would show up to town and ask questions and would want to meet us, but mountain bikers have a short memory. The best result was the *New Times* article and that only occurred because my friend Chef Todd lived next to the editor and convinced him to run the story. They sent the music editor to do the story because they figured the sports editor was too much of a jock to get along with us. He must have been really pissed when the article won sports article of the year. We treated the music editor right and took him on a club ride Sedona-style, which included swimming in Oak Creek, blackberry picking, and a slog down an irrigation aqueduct on mountain bikes. In other words, we tired him out without killing him. He had never ridden a mountain bike before and performed admirably and had the time of his life. As the Sedona 5 drifted off into oblivion, we discovered new places to ride.

ALONG THE BIKAPELLI TRAIL

One of those places was Bootleg Canyon, right next to Las Vegas, and in full view of Lake Mead on one side and Vegas on the other. We hooked up with Brent Thompson, a local artist and mountain biker extreme. Brent had gone through heart bypass surgery and his doctor suggested gardening for therapy. His yard was ultra small, and was all gardened up in a matter of weeks, so he moved his therapy up the road to Bootleg Canyon, where he turned gardening into trail-building. Brent began without official authorization, and created the Mother Trail, which would be the beginning of an exciting trail system. Brent had been to Sedona to ride with me after hearing about the Sedona 5 adventure, and made me promise to visit his new mountain bike paradise.

Bootleg does not contain the raw beauty of Sedona, but was prime terrain for mountain bikers, big-horned sheep, desert tortoises, and a golf course. It was a ratty, ragged, rugged, desert landscape, not conducive to much of anything, but the terrain was ready for mountain bikers who only need trails or visions of trails to be used. That first trip included me, Dan Diaz and his girlfriend, rider extraordinaire, Amy. This was way before Bootleg Canyon became the major downhill mountain bike mecca that it is today. It turned out that Amy was one of, if not the first, woman to venture onto the mountain on a bike, and Brent couldn't believe all the stuff she rode. We had an amazing trip and became some of Brent's earliest supporters. For years to come, Bootleg Canyon became a regular riding spot along the Bikapelli Trail. We even helped build trails there.

One year the town decided to build a golf course just below the Mother Trail. Somehow Brent was able to leverage that golf course project into sanctioned development of a huge trail system on the mountain. Rumor has it that he threatened to stop the golf course development over some endangered cactus, and was able to get a paying job to build trails. We would regularly ride Bootleg on our way to Interbike, before it became the home for the tradeshow's dirt demo. In those early years, we rarely made it to the Blue Diamond ride area for the dirt demo, instead, opting to play at Bootleg. I do remember going there with a large contingent of Sedonans and doing a magic night ride, which Brent immortalized on one of his famous block prints. As Bootleg became more downhill-oriented, it lost some of its appeal for me, and I went off in search of new adventure spots.

That's how we came to hook up with Dean Williamson, one of the creators of the Zion area trail system. Again, we rode with Dean in Sedona, before we headed up to his neck of the woods. We brought a large crew and video cameras to boot. We decided it was time to develop our own mountain bike travel show called *Along the Bikapelli Trail*. While in Sedona, Dean had broken his ankle doing some silly wheelie drop, and he was still wearing the cast. This was not the first time a gnarly mountain biker had worn a cast while biking with us. Our first such experience was reserved for one of our very own original gnarly dudes, Jules First Blood. I guess the tough just keep going.

When we arrived in Zion, we stopped by Dean's bike shop in Springdale, just outside of Zion National Park, called, as you may have guessed, Bike Zion. When we got there, he was in the process of putting on some wimpy-looking, new front tire that someone had sent him for free. We couldn't figure out why anyone would put something that wimpy on their bike, and I guess we knew what we were talking about. On our first warm-up ride, Dean rolled that tire off his rim and knocked himself senseless. And I do mean senseless! We were in the middle of a loop called Slikrock Swamp, when he slid off a rock and hit the rock with his head. We had no idea where we were on the loop, and Dean was so disoriented, he couldn't figure it out either. We finally decided to turn back and retrace our route. Most likely, that was the longer option, and we started to run out of daylight. We sent Simon ahead to the cars and come and pick Dean up. It took him so long that the rest of us decided to pedal back to the cars as well, and we left Dangerous Dave with Dean. After all, Dangerous was a doctor of sorts, and we figured that he was best equipped to deal.

When we finally got back up the hill to where Dean and Dangerous were, it was dark, and Dean was transplanting dead cactus into the middle of the trail and then watering them with his CamelBak. We tried to get Dean into one of the vehicles, but he would have none of that, pointing out that he wanted to follow what appeared to be the North Star. Don't get me wrong, that star may have been the way to get to his house, or more likely his home, but in all honesty, it looked up to me. We finally got Dean to call his girlfriend, Patsy, who drove out and picked him up, and led us to the sanctity of their home where we made dinner and relaxed.

Dean was pretty beaten up from that crash and needed to have his lip stitched up. Those stitches were installed by a slightly inebriated, I mean very inebriated, nurse at about one in the morning. We were sure that Dean would not be up to riding the next day, but we were wrong, and he was up bright and early the next morning. The first thing we made him do was to put the old tire back on the front of his bike; at least it was beefy. That day we played on some of Dean's favorite trails, and we had the cameras rolling to catch his next encounter with the dirt. This time it wasn't nearly as bad, and hardly made a dent in his demeanor, although it did make a dent in the earth.

On our last day in Zion, we found the Tree of Mystery and convinced Dangerous Dave to roll the dead tree and jump off the end with his bike. Seriously, it didn't take much convincing. In the video of this shoot, we used the old Green Hornet rendition of the *Flight of the Bumblebee*. This was our first video production, and we used two cameras and had a great time making it. I ran one camera, and Georgeous George, one of the shop guys, ran the other one. We weren't the crazy bike riders in the group, and probably wouldn't have added much entertainment value to the video anyway.

Our next—and last—video adventure took us to Red Canyon, also in Utah. Several years earlier we had set up an outpost bike shop in Panguitch Utah, which was manned by Crazy Steve. This is in the heart of Bryce Canyon, Red Canyon, Panguitch Lake, and a short distance from Brianhead. For this shoot, we had four cameras rolling and by now we had a much better idea of what looked good on film. During this video shoot, we caught Simon having an amazing crash, narrowly escaping getting whacked real hard by his bike. Josh pulled off a very nice jump, and Dangerous Dave showed everyone how to do impossible switchbacks. The scariest sequence showed Georgeous, again on the camera, getting whacked in the head by a Cannondale bike. Lucky for him, he had his helmet on! This video highlighted some of the great riding we did out of the Panguitch location, but it probably wasn't our gnarliest, most exciting Utah ride experience.

That has to be reserved for the Brianhead to Spruce Mountain route, in which we almost lost The NOD in a herd of elk. This was a long day of riding, and using Crazy Steve as the trail guide is always a risk in itself. The Brianhead part was not so bad, even though we did one of the gnarliest trails off the mountain, the old Dark Hallow trail, which took us to the Panguitch Lake area. From there, we had to do a bit of trail-finding to link up the Spruce Mountain segment. During that part, The NOD went exploring on his own and ended up in the middle of a pack of elk. It took him over an hour to catch back up to the rest of the group, and we were standing still. It only goes to show that one wrong turn can lead to big problems. The ride, itself, was very long and we ended up pedaling into town in the cold and dark. We all had a fine day, and The NOD had stories of elk to tell about.

One year there was a hotshot kid named DR and his quieter buddy, Mark. We rode many rides together and pioneered a few routes Rama-style. One of our most unique adventures was in Walker Basin. Instead of using the trail, we decided to head down a wash. We rode down this wash until we came upon a 100-foot drop with a pool of water at its bottom. By that time, it was getting dark and we ended up leaving our bikes and scurrying up the steep sides of the wash to bale out for the night. It was easy to find the road that our truck was parked on, but because it was a moonless night, we preceded to walk right past the truck. The next day, we headed back to retrieve our bikes. The boys were way ahead and got to the bikes before me. When they got there, they began throwing rocks down into the water below. Boys will be boys, and they were still throwing rocks when I got there. I sat down on a ledge overlooking the wash and peeled an orange, and when I looked up across the wash, a wall of petroglyphs was staring back at me. It depicted the story of the watering hole with glyphs of the water, animals and hunters that had shut down our ride. That was a way cool spot that I have never made it back to.

Perhaps, Sedona's greatest times were the Verde Valley School concerts. Within two or three weeks of each other, every year, we were treated to Jazz on the Rocks and the Jackson Browne Scholarship Concert. As mountain bikers, we had it made. A short ride to the creek, a water crossing at Red Rock Crossing, and a techy scurry around the Verde Valley School on unused horse trails to get up on the rocks behind the concert. Here we would join the non-bikers and everyone would rock out to the music. You just can't beat a sunny afternoon grooving in and on the rocks listening to the music vibrate off the red rocks of Cathedral Rock. 911 marked the year that the Jackson Browne show ended. My favorite show over all those years has to have been when Neil Young brought the Crazy Horse Band and they grunged out well past the noise curfew. Jazz on the Rocks had already been moved to the Cultural Park, which was in the midst of its short life. As time has gone on, Jazz on the

Rocks has re-established itself and is still a great Sedona happening, but the Jackson Browne show never happened again.

Speaking of concerts, one trip Old Doc Bill and I went to Angel Fire in New Mexico. It was the year that the Rainbow Gathering was happening just down the road a few hours, and Angel Fire was sponsoring a One World Music Festival. We had brought our bikes and spent the day riding around the ski mountain. Doc had only ridden in Sedona, which has loose rocks and he kept saying, "I can't ride on these stationary rocks." In the afternoon, we were sitting down listening to the music, when security personnel on horseback startled us. These guys snuck up on us in such a way that we didn't see them until they were right next to us. We were sure they were about to kick us out, but we were to be even more surprised as to what happened next. They were extremely friendly towards us because of the mountain bikes, saying they had their own bikes at home. After speaking with us, the security folks looked up the hill and proceeded to tell all the hippies to move on. They turned back to us and said, "Have a great time," and then they were gone. It was so unreal that it felt like a dream. That was the day I determined that mountain bikers were one rung up on the social ladder from hippies, but only one rung!

Full-moon rides are a special experience. They are hard for me because they screw up my schedule. I am an early-to-bed, early-to-rise type of guy. When I do make it on those rides, they are always worth it and I have a great time. Johnny and Dangerous do full-moon rides every month regardless of the weather. Sometimes I go along, sometimes others go along, but these two guys always go. One ride that

I didn't go on turned into quite an ordeal. The ride was in the Casner Mountain area and turned into an epic death march. Johnny, Dangerous, and Gabe each ran out of water, saw a bear, and ended up having to leave their bikes in a wash to be retrieved the next day. This ride, as I understand, had several ominous warnings. First off, the shuttle vehicle had a flat and had to be fixed even before the ride got started. Warning number two was from the spirit trying it's hardest. Get this, Johnny goes and opens an antique Bible that Dangerous had out on display, and the words he reads are "though shall not set foot upon the mountain." The universal spirit was really trying its hardest, but the gnarly crew dudes were just not paying any heed. After running out of water and hike-a-biking down a wash for hours, the boys left their bikes in the wash, found the truck, and headed home. They were out for twelve hours, were hammered, dehydrated and delirious, and still had to go back the next day for their bikes. That was one full-moon ride I was glad that I missed.

NODS AND NODDESSES

Sedona is not a young people's town. It is an artisan's community and a retirement community gone new age. Of course, mountain bikers come in all ages, shapes, and sizes. But it seems that the Mountain Bike Heaven ride community is skewed towards the older end of the age spectrum as far as mountain bikers go. With that in mind, we have developed a group called the Nods and Noddesses. Since there are very few official rewards for mountain biking, we created our own, which is based solely on age. Once you have reached fifty years old, assuming that you are still riding your mountain bike, you have achieved Nodhood or Noddesshood. This is the acronym for gnarly old dude and its female counterpart. I know, you're thinking gnarly starts with a G, but we had to avoid the inflated heads that would result from calling ourselves gods and goddesses, and besides, that is just a little bit too new age for mountain bikers.

The original Nod, we call The NOD. He is a short, somewhat stout Native American who is as tough as it comes. At first, he was one of the only over-fifty aged riders, but nowadays he has lots of company. As we have gotten older, we have had to use Super Nod and Super Duper Nod to distinguish age. Currently, Rodger is the reigning Super Duper Nod, over seventy years of age, and still shredding strong.

Each year or so, we have a new Nod who is called the Youngest Nod. I had that honor for about three years before I was relieved of the moniker by StevieB, and then by Tim.

Recently, this honor seems to change hands more frequently. Amp was recently replaced by Simon, who was then replaced by Dean. One thing is for sure: we all get older each year and it's only through our mountain biking that we stay young at heart.

There are so many Nods in Sedona that we have an informal Nodfest. After threatening to have one for years, we finally did. As of this writing, we have just had our eleventh annual Nodfest on 11-11-11. After all, who's counting anyway? Next year's twelfth annual Nodfest will be held on 12-12-12, but it's anyone's guess as to where. One thing is for certain: if the planet is destroyed, I'm pretty sure that the Nods will survive.

Our reigning Super Noddess is Judy from California, and our reigning local Noddess is Janet. The youngest Noddess is Debbie. I only mention the names, because this group of riders deserves our utmost of respect. The NOD has been my hero forever, and even though I am much younger, I certainly have no illusions that I will ever be as tough as he is. My hat is off to all the Nods and Noddesses, for without you, I would have no one but young people to ride with.

SHOPCAT

Another one of Mountain Bike Heaven's heroes was Shopcat. Although we have had several cats over the years, there will be only one official Shopcat. This cat was given to us when he was very young because he kept beating up his brother. He would end up strangling his brother until he passed out. He was a smallish black cat and he arrived towards the evening one day. We kept him in that night, but the next day, the doors of the shop were wide open, and the little black cat ran in and out like he owned the place, and from that point on, he did. Mountain Bike Heaven was right on 89A, and we never knew how long a cat could last that close to the highway. Shopcat lasted close to decade, finally using up all his nine lives. The bike shop was never the same after his death, but we struggled on for many years using substitutes that never seemed to last very long before disappearing. I am hopeful that they all found good homes. Shopcat's exploits were known far and wide, and he even became one of Mountain Bike Heaven's most popular logos. He appears on hats, t-shirts, and stickers, and even ended up on my calf as an elaborate tattoo, as well as the cover of this book.

One of his most notable accomplishments occurred in the backyard of the shop. Shopcat was a voracious hunter, and by that time, he had rid the yard of pretty much everything that moved. On this particular day, he was spotted high up in the biggest tree in the yard fighting off a big raven. He climbed the large tree and literally took the raven out of the sky. They tumbled down through the branches, and Shopcat was victorious. The story was pieced together through various sightings throughout the day, and culminated when a customer said, "Do you know that your cat has a huge black bird in the clothing area with its head missing?"

I remember in the early days when he would bring in lizards, I would take them away and throw them on the roof. Somehow, within minutes he would be back with that lizard. I found out that he would use the trees in the front of the shop to climb up on the roof and reclaim possession of his prize. Sometimes he would just climb on the roof and trick customers into thinking he couldn't get off. On numerous occasions, I'd have concerned customers come in, all in a panic, saying that "your cat is stuck on the roof." Of course, he was only playing with them. I would then go out back and position one of the shed doors so he could get on top and walk down the door like it was a ramp. Sometimes he would end up inside people's cars if they left their door open or their windows open, and one time he took a short crazy ride on the top of Simon's truck. That day, Simon was heading to Cottonwood but had to get gas first. When he stopped, just a few blocks from the shop, he found Shopcat hunkered down with his claws out holding on for dear life. When Simon brought Shopcat back, he commented, "I was wondering what that strange noise was." I doubt he would have made it the whole way to Cottonwood, especially the way that Simon drives.

Shopcat will live on in infamy after all the logoed gear has come and gone, or at least until I pass away. After all, anyone riding behind me has a bird's-eye view of him on my tattooed calf.

MAX THE RUNAWAY DOG

Max, the Brittany Spaniel, came into my life one day. His human caretakers no longer had the time for him, and I was lucky enough to be chosen as his new human friend. I would see him dragging this hefty lady up the hill past my mom's house on his morning walk and would be reminded of my childhood friend. One day his human mom had enough and asked around if anyone wanted a dog. My friend, Julia Dear, was the massage therapist for Max's mom, and she remembered that I had had a Brittany Spaniel growing up. The rest is history, and Max and I have been together for almost a decade.

Simon had brought dogs on the rides years ago, but dogs had not been part of the gnarly crew for quite some time. That was all about to change. It took Max three rides before he got the ride concept. The first ride, he ran away with his leash attached right at the beginning. The second ride, I kept him leashed for the entire ride. By the third ride, I had had enough and figured if he couldn't figure this ride stuff out, then he wasn't going to be a mountain bike dog. Well, off the leash he went, and he stayed more or less on the ride. He didn't stick to the trail per se, but ran along in the woods in the same general direction as we were going.

Brittanies are hunting dogs and are traditionally used as flushers. So, Max felt the urge to look under every bush to make sure there wasn't something there for him to flush out. When he did find something, he was off on the chase; with his yelp of, I found something trailing off in the distance. All the other ride dogs stay on the trail, close to their humans, but Max runs to a different beat. He runs with us, sort of, but he is also known as the dog that constantly runs away. He can always find his way back, but he usually doesn't care to, and I've spent many an hour after the ride searching or waiting for him to find his way out of the woods.

On more than one occasion, he has found a different group of riders, with or without dogs, and has found his way home that way. Over the years, he has spent the night in some pretty ritzy digs waiting for me to pick him up the next day. He has even had to spend the night in doggy jail a few times. As he has gotten older, he still runs away, but when found, he looks so tired and pitiful that even the police bring him home rather than off to doggy jail. When people see him lounging around the bike shop, they can't believe he is a mountain biking dog, but after they have had the opportunity of riding with him, they are always amazed at how much ground he covers.

Like many dogs in Sedona, Max has had his run-ins with the wild pigs, known as javelina. He has been gored a few times and has been lucky enough to survive to run again another day. One day, I went hiking with him and that day we drove to the hike spot. He did his usual runaway game, and after waiting an hour for him to return, I had to go to work at the bike shop. A couple of hours later, I got a call from someone who recognized him, and he was in town, a short distance from the bike shop. He had found his way back into town by taking one of the many mountain bike trails that he knew. At that point, I realized that Max could find his way back from anywhere in Sedona, if he wanted to.

Because of Max's proclivity to run away, we decided to create a special dog ride, in the hopes that he might stick

Ramajon

around if there were more doggy friends around. It kind of worked, but not always. Brittanies, as a breed, are very independent, and they think that they are much smarter than humans. He's probably right! The dog rides became very popular for mountain bikers with dogs, and on one occasion, we had thirteen dogs along and only eight riders. No, dogs didn't just show up without riders; it turns out that many dog owners have more than one dog that likes to mountain bike.

Max has been my inspiration and has helped keep me riding. Sometimes it's hard to get out and ride. Lack of desire and motivation is always a thing that we deal with in our daily lives. So, feeling responsible as a dog owner to exercise Max has kept me going out riding even on those days that I feel uninspired. It usually takes me an hour or longer to get into the flow, so watching that little cropped tail wag back and forth as he runs through the woods has been an inspiration even on those days I just didn't want to go.

Of course, with Max, I may not get to see him very much on the ride, but I know he's out there following his own inner guidance and having a great time. And I know that he will eventually find his way out of the woods, with or without me. Lately he has opted to hitch rides back into town. After running for five or six hours non-stop, he looks pretty tired, and as he has gotten older, he has been able to use the pity aspect to get unsuspecting trail users to call the number on his tag and get me to come and pick him up. Just the other day, he had some older lady fawning over him as he lay in her backyard feigning an inability to move. I think he was hoping for a steak dinner. Between Max and myself, we have covered more ground in Sedona's red rocks, both on and off trail, than any other trail users. For many years I thought Max was just following his heart or his nose when he disappeared off of the trails, but one day I was reminded by one of my longtime mounain biker friends that Max was simply following my example.

TRAIL DEVELOPMENT ETIQUETTE

In the early days, we rode existing trails or Rama routes where we never moved a rock or branch from the trail. Everything was so fresh and new that we didn't have to. Many of those early trails simply came into existence by people following along behind me on the club rides. As we got into better shape and technology allowed for more extreme riding, we spent more time riding. A need began to develop for longer trails and to go into places that hadn't been as thoroughly explored. Our early explorations were simply cross-country routes, but at some point, people felt a need for more than just a faint Rama ride route.

Enter in the trail-building phase of Sedona's development. Some of the trail developers came from afar, while others were long-term Sedona residents. At first it was a desire to smooth out the older routes, but then a big shift happened. New trails started sprouting up everywhere. Many of these new routes were established in some of Sedona's roughest and toughest terrain. Others were in areas that just had a ton of unused open space. Regardless, this phase of development added to a long neglected desire for more and longer trails. We had become better riders, we were in better shape, and new technology allowed for mountain bikers to ride in places that before would have been considered unrideable. In addition, there is an innate human desire to make an impact on nature. The manifest destiny of mountain biking was upon us, a desire to remake nature in a more rideable manner. The age of trail developers was here, and boy did they do an incredible job.

One of the first places that got opened up was off of Mitten Ridge. Prior to trail development, this area was virtually unused, unrideable, and a nasty hike-a-bike to boot. Our first attempt at conquering this terrain was dubbed Loma Casi by Dawn, and resulted in a typical death-march type of hike-a-bike. The newly developed trails in this area include Damnifiknow, Damnifudo, Damnifudont, Killer Bee, Levitra, Sic Rock and, perhaps the most impressive of all, Hangover. These trails are some of the most extreme trails in Sedona and have become very popular and are now favorites of hikers and bikers both local and out-of-towners who want to challenge themselves.

Broken Arrow is another area that was greatly enhanced by the trail-development movement. These trails were so much fun that homeowners wanted them for themselves, and for a time, battled the mountain bikers for control. Of course, that turned into a losing battle, and these trails have become another favorite spot for mountain bikers. These trails are named after an unlikely animal, with names like Hog Heaven, High on the Hog, Hog Wash, Hogalicious, and Pig Tail.

Cathedral Rock also gained new trails, with one of Sedona's most amazing creations, Highline. This trail took close to three years to complete and was built virtually single-handedly. The other new trails in the Cathedral Rock area are: Made in the Shade, Slim Shady, and the Easy Breezy Sleazys. These trails take the classic Sedona approach and use the washes very effectively.

It seems that every area gained new trails during this era. The first new trail to appear in Carrol Canyon was Windsurfer, shortly followed by Bogus, and then, one of the most ridden trails in all of Sedona, Sketch. Other connector trails soon appeared like Upper Rams Head, Lemonade, Cakewalk, and the Homeys. Close in proximity to Carrol Canyon is the Pyramid, which also gained several new trails, one of which may be the most impressive find of all time. This trail goes through some of the gnarliest terrain in town. I know, because I used to spend hours hike-a-biking in this area and would get absolutely nowhere. In one direction it is called Special Ed; in the other direction it is called Tin Can Alley. This trail is great in both directions, a feat in itself. Traveling from the high school to the Pyramid, it then hooks up with Witch Doctor on the descent off the Pyramid.

The Dry Creek Basin and the Coxcomb network also became riddled with new trails, and I do mean riddled. Many of our early trails in this area had already been adopted into the trail system, like Compactor and Snake trails. The next generations are soon to be adopted into the system: Touron, Chuckwagon, Mescal, Gunslinger, Gunsmoke, and Anaconda. Others may never become official trails. Those, of course, are everyone's favorites: Canyon of Fools, Ledge and Air, Plumbers Crack, Draino, Last Frontier, Western Civilization, and the infamous Earl's Loop.

The last main riding area is Secret Trails. "What do you do with Secret Trails?" the forest circus asked once. Our response was, "Keep them secret!" Secret Trails developed almost entirely from our Saturday Club rides twenty years ago. This area was right across from the original Mountain Bike Heaven, and every Saturday we would go riding there to break our bikes before Sunday's all-day adventure ride. Over the years, even Secret Trails grew. The addition of

Second Coming made the original Crucifixion Wash rideable for all Sedonuts, and almost rideable for most out-of-towners. The last remnant of Upper Secret Trails became Lost and Found, and these two access points are right next to each other, starting at St. John Vianney Church. Other notable new Secret Trails and trails in close proximity include Centennial, Anthill, Sloppy Biscuits, and for the truly insane riders, Skidmark.

As you can see, Sedona's trails are designed around different areas, with many connections. Some riders have names for every connector, while others just refer to the area itself and leave the route more of a mystery. Unwitting riders following behind me on the club rides scouted many of these routes out years ago. These early routes were riddled with hike-a-bikes, and this type of ride was referred to as a Rama ride. When the trail-development era arrived, most of these routes became better defined, the politically correct term is trail enhancement. Most of the routes have been adopted, or are now scheduled to be adopted into the Sedona Trail System by the forest circus. And, to tell you the truth, it is about time. After neglecting trail development for decades, the forest circus has gotten on the bandwagon. What was once called a non-system trail is now called a user-built trail. My feeling is that if the forest circus had been doing their job of responding to the needs of the trail users, especially the mountain bike community, the expansion of the long-outdated trail system could have been sanctioned from the start. Of course, it would have taken decades to develop this many trails, as evidenced by the Aerie Trail, which took over nine years to come into existence. The Aerie Trail was flagged over nine years before any work was performed to actually build it. When the building began, it took a few local trail builders less than a month to complete. well, ahead of the forest circus schedule, and before the forest circus trail crew ever showed up.

In all fairness, the forest circus did sanction a few trails over the last twenty years. Munds Wagon Trail, Herkenham, and the long-overdue trail to Cottonwood, the Lime Kiln Trail, as well as Sedona's only beginner trail, the Bell Rock Pathway. The rest of the trail development that they did was simply dumbing down the existing trails and claiming credit for them. It has taken the forest circus over twenty years to really comprehend the necessity of an expanding trail system. It's not a hard concept to realize that people want to go on new trails and see new places. Perhaps it's taken the forest circus that long to hire people who like the woods and want to get out and commune with nature, rather than simply drive around in trucks and try to enforce arbitrary limits on forest users. Okay, I may sound a bit raggy on the forest circus, but the reality is, they really have been neglectful of responding to the needs of trail users, especially the mountain bike community. I know, I've witnessed the process, and have seen the real discrimination, and have been the focus of it for more than two decades. Don't get me wrong; I may have deserved it, but if I had done half of what I have been accused of, I would have been worse than Jesse James and Bonnie and Clyde combined.

The best example of the discrimination is related to the mountain bike tour guide permit. I can't even begin to count how many mountain bikers came to Sedona with a dream to cooperate with the forest circus to obtain legal tour permits.

After all, the jeep tour operators got what they wanted, and had tour permits for decades. Matter of fact, the jeep tour business may be what made Sedona the place to visit. As each of these new mountain bikers came to town and spoke to me wondering why we didn't offer mountain bike tours, I would explain reality to them. At that point, they would look at me like I was crazy and was just negative towards the forest circus. A month later, they would stop by again, after dealing with the forest circus, all angry and frustrated, and I would seem like the voice of moderation. I knew, because I had tried the process years before, and had found that the forest circus had simply violated all their own rules and guidelines in the hope that the mountain bikers would disappear. Well, guess what, we just kept multiplying and the forest circus had to finally make some accommodations for mountain bike tours. But I tell you, if they had applied that same process to the jeep tours, we wouldn't have a Pink Jeep Tour business today!

THE UNUSUAL SUSPECTS

No mountain bike book on Sedona would be complete without including a section on the mountain bike characters themselves, all the unusual suspects. If I leave someone out, please don't feel slighted; it's just that I have attracted so many strange characters over so many years that I simply can't remember all of you at one time. It also leaves things open for another book.

Wheelie Todd was one of the fastest mountain bikers to ever end up in Sedona. He was a great bike handler, liked playing in the obstacles, liked jumping off and over things, and was a great mechanic. He worked at Mountain Bike Heaven for many years and developed deep friendships with many customers, who would ask about him years later.

Wheelie had a long history with bikes: from his early days as a BMX racer to NYC loading dock jumping, to winning an Arizona Expert Class Cross-Country Championship. Matter of fact, if I didn't know better, I'd say he was born in a bike shop from the union of two bikes. He had a love for racing and riding, but couldn't wrap his head around the idea of training. For him it was all about natural ability and riding and riding fast. The year he won the AZ State Expert Cross-Country Championship was the year he commuted to and from Cottonwood every day. It had nothing to do with training; he was just commuting. In those days, when he did train, it would be crazy things like doing a 100-mile ride the day before a race. He truly liked the idea and actuality of working in a bike shop, and to this day, even while working a real full time job in construction, he always finds time to work a day in a bike shop.

The strangest mountain biker to ever land in Sedona, and that is saying a lot, has to have been The Mattster. Mattster is one of those people that needed mountain biking to keep from hurting himself or others. He was an ornery old man before his time, and the Red Rock trails may have been the only thing that made him forget about how tough life is in general and his life specifically. He was a production framer, a mountain bike addict, and probably a drug addict as well. As I've said before, some mountain bikers would be a danger to themselves and society if they didn't ride. Mattster had a hard life and a hard job, and his body ached every moment of every day. For him, mountain biking was the only real release he ever had. Perhaps meditation would have helped The Mattster, but that would have required too much effort or too little effort depending upon your perception, and besides, meditation forces you to face yourself, while mountain biking only requires that you get on a bike and pedal.

Mattster was probably the original gnarly old dude, and should be credited with coming up with the term. Of course, at the time, he was only in his forties and was immediately disqualified because he was not over fifty yet. While in Sedona, Mattster laid down a couple of super gnarly descents off of Cry Baby Mountain that were so gnarly that most of us including him couldn't ride them. After lying dormant for many years, these routes may once again get some action from those seeking the ultra gnarly if they have the fortitude to find them. Mattster may not have been the fastest rider, but one thing was for sure: he was game to

Ramajon

follow me on any Rama ride no matter how gnarly it was. Just looking at The Mattster made you think of gnarly. He had scraggly, long hair, a gold cap on one of his front teeth, and a darkish, sun-baked complexion from working out in the elements for so many years. He also spoke in a kinda raspy voice with a ghetto dialect. He was just plain scary.

Another framer showed up along with Mattster. He was an elite racer named Big Brian. He dealt with his pain in a different way, but you could tell that he had it. Brian was a tall guy that had the longest legs on the planet. To this day, he was one of the fastest, most technically inclined riders to ride with us. Because he was incredibly skilled at obstacles and jumping off of things, he starred in the TLC (The Learning Channel) video that was shot in Sedona. When the video was aired, the riders were showcased right after the crazy people who rode a huge log down a steep hill, and that made mountain biking seem tame in comparison. But, trust me, mountain biking in Sedona is anything but tame, although as the years have gone by, the trails have been tamed.

Around this same time, there was a young crazy named DR. He was mostly talk, but when put to the test, he was actually quite a skilled rider. I rode with him quite a bit during the one season he was in town. The Bike Path to the High School trail was one that we rode into existence Rama-style, without moving a rock or breaking a branch. This kid was trouble and he may have been involved in one of the Mountain Bike Heaven robberies. He wanted to be respected as a downhill racer more than anything in the world, but he was just a bit too flaky to be consistent. He did, however, have his moment of glory during the shooting of one of the early Cranked movies. They were setting up a shoot of a couple of riders coming out of a cave way up on Mescal Mountain. The problem was that DR was so cranked up that he couldn't wait for the cameraman to give him the go-ahead and instead jumped the gun. DR and the other rider, who was going to be the star of the movie, bolted out of the cave before the cameras were even set, and disaster struck. The star ended up by getting into terrain that was too much and sprained his ankle. The unfortunate thing was that it was the first day of shooting, and the star was lost. DR never made it into that video, but several other bike shops confirmed that they thought he had been involved in robberies of their shops too.

Robert is the closest thing I have seen to a real master in Sedona and on the bike rides. Not a master of riding per se, but a master of the occult for lack of a better word. He is not the type of master who brags about their mastery and wisdom, but a regular quiet guy who holds a lot of wisdom in his heart and works in realms that the rest of us can only dream about. He is so well versed in the spiritual arts that it always amazes me when he tells me about his latest adventure or field of study. When I really need a healing, he is the only one that I trust and go to. He sees and experiences realms that I wouldn't believe even exist, except for the fact that when he tells me about them, I somehow know they are real. I'm glad I don't have to be bothered by all those realms, but am very grateful that someone as knowledgeable as Robert exists, and is someone who I can call family. He was one of my earliest mountain bike friends and, in the old days, I would always love to get him talking during the breaks on the mountain bike rides. He would hold us all spellbound during those breaks, and I would love watching the out-of-towners stare wide-eyed and in awe during his stories, and I was right there with them. As I've said, Robert is very versed in old school wisdom, new school wisdom, mountain bike wisdom, and has quite a collection of mountain bikes and energy machines that do who knows what. Of all the mountain bikers I have attracted over the years, Robert has expanded my consciousness the most. He doesn't often ride with the group anymore, mostly because the group energy gets him so energized that he tries to do things on the bike he has no business doing and ends up worse for wear.

When I think of beauty in motion, I think of Roxanne. We met her by chance one day while we were out on our Sunday club ride. We were riding, and she was running with her dogs. It turned out that Roxanne was quite a mountain biker, as well as a runner, a soccer player, and a downhill skier. After that first encounter, she became a regular on our Sunday club ride and, like the rest of us, these rides became our addiction, our spiritual practice and religious service all in one. She was fit, fast, full of finesse, and a heck of a lot smarter than the rest of us, having graduated from Princeton University where she had been the captain of the cycling team. None of us had been the captain of anything, and I was more of a ringleader than a captain.

Besides being a great cross-country rider, Roxanne was a fearless downhiller as well. I remember seeing her and Simon ride down some super gnarly line of Slickrock off of Roller Coaster Proper back in the days before there were many female mountain bikers who would even consent to ride with us. The sport was young in those days, and it and we were a lot gnarlier, and we had a reputation that tended to scare both male and female mountain bikers away, except Canadian women who were a lot gnarlier than Canadian men back then.

Roxanne must have had some sort of death wish deep inside, which she extended to her personal life by always getting involved with bad boys. Troubled youth, so to speak, and I consider mountain bikers of all ages troubled youths. Perhaps it's because mountain biking keeps us young, or at least thinking young. Roxanne was a truly amazing person as well as an incredible cross-country racer. During the year that we had our race team, Roxanne walked away with two Arizona State Expert Cross-Country Championships, or should I say, pedaled away with. Her most satisfying victory, at least to me, was one in which she broke her chain and was about to toss in the hat DNF (Did Not Finish). I could tell she was disappointed, and then it dawned on me that the race was almost over and she could still win it if she ran her bike in. Being the runner and competitor that she was, it didn't take much convincing to get her to shoulder her bike and run it to the finish line. We ran along beside her to the finish line cheering her on, and she actually won the race. After she left Sedona, Roxanne ended up running the mountain bike program at Mt. Snow Vermont, which was billed as the first mountain bike school and one of the largest ski mountains turned mountain bike mecca. To quote Joe Glickman, one of her students from that era, in describing his teacher, "Roxanne Prescott is an effervescent Princeton grad with a silky DJs voice and so many scars on her muscular appendages that I wondered if she'd worked in a zoo." That describes Roxanne to a tee, and no, she hadn't worked in a zoo, only rode with the animals.

Trouble showed up one year from Long Island. His brother had gotten to Sedona first, but Trouble was the real mountain biker of the family. Trouble was a regular rider for many years. Besides his name, his claim to fame was that he started the trend of the forty-five-pound Sedona trail bike. Those years had manufacturers making longer travel and solider bikes. They may have been heavy to hike-a-bike, but when you pointed them down, they literally flew over everything. Six, seven, eight-inch travel trail bikes became the norm. Trouble earned his name by—you guessed it—causing trouble. One day he had just caused a new round of trouble and I was talking to Roxanne. We were talking about his latest exploit and we simultaneously said that boy is Trouble. We looked at each other and the rest is history and another nickname was born.

Cafinator is a tall redhead who, as you may have guessed, loves coffee. He is a true coffee connoisseur. He knows how to roast beans and brews a wicked cup of Joe. One day we were on a Mingus ride with a bunch of Canadian Nods. Cafinator was along and he had a couple of mishaps. They didn't faze him much at the time, and he just kept going. At the end of the ride, the blood was pretty awesome and he earned his moniker Cafinator. Since he is such a coffee junky, the name has stuck and he uses it today.

One of the oddest mountain bikers to grace our mountain bike community with his presence was the Terrapin Hound. This guy was loud and obnoxious, slow to get ready for the rides, and slow on the rides. But he did have an uncanny ability, and that was as a tracker. Many of our rides in that era included cross-country riding, over hill and dale, through washes and avoiding any semblance of trail or road. We would pedal away from the Terrapin Hound and head out in some unknown area, but we could never lose the dude. Whenever we were ready to break, no matter where we ended up, he would turn up from a different direction. This would happen over and over on the ride, and we never figured out how he was able to find us.

One of my favorite people in the whole of our ageless mountain bike community is Mike Bauer. He has been riding forever and over the years has consistently shown up for the club rides. He is Sedona's foremost architect, and he may have the best sense of humor on the planet. He has used his bike to commute to and from work for decades, and is an old-time Boulder Colorado roadie. If there is one person who should be Sedona's mayor, it is Mike Bauer. Our town would be a significantly better place to live in, and a lot more fun, if Mike were our mayor.

Amp showed up on a club ride one day and was hooked from the start. There is something about finding a group of mountain bikers that just want to ride and have fun that seems to attract more and more participants. Of course, for some, the constant "headset adjustments" seem to help quite a bit. Amp was one of those! He even tried to share some nasty, scruffy bottom of the CamelBak weed with us on that first ride, which really didn't help endear him to the group. Matter of fact, that and being so "amped up" made us question what his motives might have been, especially since he immediately began asking around if anyone could get him weed. Lucky for him, we ignored those negative signs and let his love of riding, and riding hard become his moniker. Right off the bat, he took to Dangerous and followed him off of every obstacle. They became a Monkey See Monkey Do duo. The one problem was that Amp landed much harder and was constantly breaking bike parts. I don't mean small parts either; I mean big, non-fixable-type repairs that we found a way of fixing. In his first four months of gnarly crew Sedona riding, he broke his East Coast Fat Chance hardtail frame three times and had to have it welded back together by Long Tall, which in itself is a perilous thing.

On one instance, we were way away from town in a wash and Danger did one of his patented jumps that he was barely able to get to. Amp, of course, followed him and landed it no problem except that he broke his crank arm off, still attached to his clip-in pedal. Well, that was the end of Amp's ride and he had to scale the side of this huge wash to get to a road and hitch a ride back into town. That wasn't the first or last time Amp had to head back home with a broken bike and his tail tucked between his legs. But it never stopped him from showing back up after his bike got put back together.

Amp is a tough guy and even tougher on his equipment. He is a construction dude and is extremely fit. Those guys who do manual labor for a living have a huge advantage on the bike rides. The rest of us have to actually train to stay fit or do exercise or calisthenics. He is a monster! Every ride he says, "I'm going to take it easy today," but the moment the ride starts, he is out front and stays there until he runs out of steam, which is hardly ever. On those rare days that I spot a weakness in Amp, I will always take advantage of it and try my hardest to put the hammer down. He is very respectful of me on those days and loves telling stories of those few and far-between rides when Rama laid the hammer down. It's funny because he always points to my sixth sense of knowing when he is at his weakest. I'd have to say that one of the best things about getting out of the bike biz is not having to repair Amp's bike anymore.

My absolute favorite visitors to Sedona are Mark and Judy. This couple lives in Marin County, and has been visiting Sedona, every year, for at least twenty years. We call them The Mark and Judy Show. They have brought many friends to Sedona over the years and liked coming here so much that they bought a house. They say the house was bought for their daughter, but I think they bought it so they would have a comfortable place to stay when they came to town, and having their daughter in town just gave them another reason for visiting. Very convenient, and Sedona is a great place to live, even if you don't mountain bike.

One year StevieB showed up in town. Even though he was a New Yorker, he came from the Santa Cruz area, and was a bike shop person from way back, and also quite a frisbee tosser as well. He had a unique connection to us, having managed a Santa Cruz bike shop, which one of our sales reps had worked in. That rep, Johnny Theus, ended up dropping out and becoming a bread baker in a spiritual community back in the Santa Cruz area. StevieB's greatest mountain bike skill is to be able to ride just a few times a year and not be out of shape. This always amazes me, because I am always struggling to be in shape, and I ride week after week, year after year. StevieB also created the slogan "Hail Thrombo" when fixing flat tires. Thrombo in

StevieB's words is the God of compressed air and, without giving the proper respect, may result in additional flat tires.

Some of the mountain bikers who have played with us have passed on. So, this is in memory of Boyscout Bob. He passed away before his time due to, of all things, chewing too many toothpicks. He was a determined rider and was always prepared for any circumstance. One time, when some hikers kept putting rocks in the middle of Mystic Trail, he snuck up on them and was able to actually photograph them in action. It turned out to be one of his neighbors, and I'm sure that went over well when he confronted them with the photos. Bob, I hope you're smiling down on us from over the rainbow.

Don Troutman had a major influence on the development of the early Sedona mountain bike scene. He owned the Dessert Quail Inn, which attracted a higher class of mountain bikers, ones who could actually afford to stay in a hotel. One of his main connections was with Ralph Hines, who was one of the principles behind Proflex. Within no time at all, we had the Proflex race team training in Sedona. For those of you who don't remember that far back, Proflex was one of the early dual-suspension manufacturers, and in those days, they were like God. Our first year selling Proflexes, we split an order with a bike shop in Flagstaff, each taking three bikes. That year, we sold thirty-six Proflex dual-suspension bikes. Of course, it helped that there was virtually no other choices that were affordable. Troutman rode quite a bit in those days, and was one of the first Nods.

Ole Doc Bill is from Detroit, Cleveland and Toronto. Doc was an old friend from my Cleveland health food store days. He had wandered into my health food store years ago and we had become immediate friends. When I came out to Sedona, Doc followed shortly and took to mountain biking like a fish takes to water. He is our sole black Nod. For those who don't know, Sedona has a ton of brown people, but only a handful of black people. I have always felt honored to have Doc as a member of the gnarly crew and have always liked the fact that we are an equal-opportunity riding group. We have had other Afro-Americans, Simon and Franny, who were both born and raised in South Africa, but Doc is the only Afro-American of color, and he is colorful, always embellishing his bikes with bling.

 I don't think Doc ever had seen a mountain bike before he got to Sedona. I take that back. One day in Cleveland, I was out on my mountain bike in a fresh snow storm when I rode past Doc, who was at the ATM machine and startled the heck out of him. I remember him saying, "You got to be crazy to ride a bike in the snow; I'll never do that!" Well, I proved him wrong; several years later after both he and I had moved to Sedona, he was out riding in the snow with the rest of us. Snow riding in Sedona is a special treat, because the snow doesn't stay around very long and the sun usually comes out in a few hours and makes the Red Rocks vibrate even more than regular.

 On our Saturday club rides, Doc would always have to leave early and would ask what the quickest way out was. Bullish Dude would always just point in the direction of 89A and say "that way." By his third ride, Doc had figured it out, and when he was ready to bale, he just started heading through the woods towards 89A. Doc was a great storyteller and would get very animated when telling mountain bike tales. One of his best stories was about a ride in Woods

Canyon. In those days, Woods Canyon was not used by anyone for anything. We rode it one day, and it was way overgrown with cats claw and huge prickly pear cactus. As Doc tells it, those huge cactuses would move in front of him and block his way every time they had the chance to. I never saw them move, but Doc's story was so convincing that I'm sure they did move to block his passage through.

Frankasaurus is a jolly old dude; he is one of the original Nods and is so old that the last group he rode with were dinosaurs. He looks at biking in a different light than anyone else. Being a mad scientist of nutritional formulas, Frankasaurus uses mountain biking as a proving ground. I'm not exactly sure what he is trying to prove, but every ride he goes on he has another secret concoction drink along. He may be trying to determine which combination gives him the most energy, speed, or endurance, or he might be trying to determine which combination tastes the worse. Over the years, I've tried quite a few of his combinations, and although I have no conclusive results about any of the above criteria, I have also never regurgitated any of his magic formulas back up. If anyone is going to discover the fountain of youth formula, it will be Frankasaurus, and he may have already done it. My conclusion is, whatever helps you ride must be part of the right combination, and if it doesn't make you puke, it's probably okay to share with others. Since Frankasaurus is still riding, it is quite possible that his concoctions really do work.

I can remember one stretch of rides where Frankasaurus kept losing suspension parts off his bike on the trail. It was the era of the Proflex rubber bumper suspension and other riders would keep coming into the bike shop with his parts and stories of finding all these suspension parts out on the trails. Fortunately, we have moved beyond the Proflex years into more complex suspensions, and Frankasaurus doesn't litter the trails with suspension parts anymore.

Frankasaurus is a very philosophical, talkative dude and it is not uncommon for us to loose him on the trail. When we, on rare occasions, go back and look for him and the other lost riders he is with, we always find him in intense conversation about God knows what. Usually they are so deep in conversation that they never even realized the group continued on. Frankasaurus travels a lot and never ever goes anywhere without his mountain bike. When you become a super or super duper Nod, you can't afford to miss any days of riding, because it is so hard to get back at it and back into shape, or it could be that you might lose track of time and forget how to ride a bike.

One mountain biker who showed up in Sedona while he was still very young was Tex. We found him one day hoppity-hopping out on Chicken Point when he was just barely a teenager. He was an urban dweller and was great at the trialsy stuff, but hadn't explored cross country mountain biking yet. He has since developed into one of the best all-around mountain bikers in Sedona. An avid racer of both cross-country and downhill venues, Tex has slimmed down over the past several years, and may be getting ready to be better than ever before. I have to mention this as a joke. The last several Squealer Races he has participated in have left him wondering why they even make those lightweight mountain bike tires. I, on the other hand, wonder why anyone as strong as Tex is even concerned with anything lightweight.

There are exceptional riders and there are exceptional riders. One such man came to Arizona to compete in our only pro-quality elite race, which was the Cactus Cup. His name was John Jenkins, and this is a short tribute to him. When he first came to ride with us, he was quiet and unassuming. He was a few years older, so at first glance, we weren't expecting him to be as tough a rider as he turned out to be. He also would wear cutoff blue jeans and had a rack on the back of his bike. All this led us to wonder, who was this weird guy from the East Coast? Of course, all riders are welcome to come along on our club rides, except whiners, and John was definitely not a whiner. No matter how hard I pedaled, I could not distance myself from John. He was always on my tail with a smile on his face and was game for anything, even waist-deep wades through Oak Creek. It turned out that John was the Mid-Atlantic Expert Masters Champion, which meant that he was a faster, more determined rider than I would ever be. There was no wonder I couldn't drop him. John is no longer with us, having passed away in a bizarre carpentry accident. I'd just like to thank his spirit for the opportunity of being able to ride with him a few times.

Along with John came another mad man mountain biker—Alaska Doug. Anyone who lives in Alaska has to be a bit crazy, and when Doug moved to Sedona years later, my suspicions were verified. Doug loves to ride, and even though he tells me he does other things in Alaska, like work, I don't believe it for a moment. He will ride day after day until he is so exhausted that he has to take a day off. I think he eventually gets to the point where he can't move, and then takes a rest day to recuperate, and then he is back riding. In his mind, as an old-time visitor and new resident, he has a lot of catching up to do. He recently purchased a great house in the Dry Creek Basin, and we use his house for before-and after-ride festivities.

When I first met Dean, I thought I had met Castro. He had a long, scraggly beard and was always dressed in military garb. By that time, Dean had already gotten into trouble for making trails near Zion National Park in Utah. He didn't really make trails, so to speak, but had marked routes on the Slickrock, and I guess that is a no-no in Utah. His punishment for making trails was community service, which consisted of making trails for the BLM or some other government authority. Somewhat ironic, I guess, but when it comes to the recreational use of the forests, it's all about control, and in Utah, the punishment for making trails is to make more trails. To Dean's credit, he took the rap for trail enhancements that he may not have been the only one doing, but he had the bike shop and was making money using the trails. Although, when he told me how little money he made in a year, I'm not sure if that really qualified as making money. But he did like being a mountain bike pioneer, and he had found a cool place to ride and had put together a pretty cool network of trail areas. It seems mountain bike pioneers attract one another, and we first met Dean when he came to Sedona to ride and ended up breaking his ankle doing some silly wheelie roll-in, but he was just being Dean. After that, we went up to Utah with the gnarly crew and rode with Dean on his home turf with his leg still in its cast.

Years later, Dean would move to Sedona, and guess what, he got into more trouble. You can take the boy out of Utah, but you can't change his ways. Trail laws are a lot different in Sedona than they are in Utah. They can try to deconstruct a trail that has been built, causing major environmental damage in the process, but it is doubtful that they can keep mountain bikers away from a trail that they want to ride. Plus, there are way more mountain bikers out there playing than there are forest circus personnel willing to get out of their trucks. It took the forest circus nearly twenty years of batting their heads against the trees before they have accepted that mountain bikers exist and are not going anywhere. They have also found that mountain bikers don't take too kindly to lip service and platitudes. Dean is one of the mountain bikers directly responsible for the shift in this attitude, and when he got into trouble in Sedona, and it wasn't for trail building, his community service was, you guessed it, trail building. It's too bad that most trail enhancers can't get paid for their work, because if there ever were someone deserving of trail development money, it would be Dean. Dean's arrival in Sedona marked a huge shift in the trail-development etiquette and emphasis. It's strange how a movement seems to shift at a moment's notice, gain steam quickly, and create a tipping point.

Before Dean made it to Sedona, he was instrumental in another mountain bike trend. That trend was to get all the mountain bike crazies to coalesce in one place to see who in fact was the best at being crazy. That event was called The Red Bull Rampage. Dean's sight location knowledge, and his notoriety, and perhaps his protégé, Bender, all led to an event that changed the face of mountain biking forever. Of course, it helped that Red Bull had a desire to dominate the energy drink market and had the money to do it. Otherwise, there never would have been a focal point for the extreme of the extreme mountain biker to do things that to most is beyond their wildest comprehension.

Anyway, after Dean got kicked out of Utah, which is quite a feat in itself, he ended up in Sedona and before long ended up working at Mountain Bike Heaven. Dean was a good-natured dude, had a penchant for trying to pick up every chick he met, not unlike Dangerous Dave, and relished giving out trail information. His trail info descriptions were so detailed it sometimes—no, every time—seemed he was describing every rock on the trail or cactus out there. I figured he never truly accepted the fact that he wasn't in Zion anymore. Although Sedona is laid-back and all, we were a heck of a lot busier than Zion, and most of the people who are given trail info, whether you spent a minute or an hour or a day giving it, always had the same question afterwards. That question was, "Which way do we go to get to the trailhead?" as they invariably point in the wrong direction. And to tell you the truth, after all these years and with the best of maps and guidebooks, riders are still out there in Sedona's Red Rocks as confused as ever. The best-laid maps of mice and men are no match for a lost mountain biker. The best analogy I have come up with over the years is to compare mountain bikers to the New Agers with the statement related to spiritual searchers. If you've ever been to Sedona and spoken to the New Agers, it is quite obvious that they are lost and no crystal, vortex, or reader is likely going to help them find themselves. Why should mountain bikers feel that they are any different! They may be closer to the Red Rocks especially when they have fallen off their bikes, but most likely they are just as lost. One of my favorite Rama-isms is if you've got your map out on the trail, you're lost already.

I deviate, back to Dean. I believe his greatest penchant is to redesign the mountain bike. He has already had an impact on redesigning what people do on a mountain bike. So, he started with the pedal. His design was to make them thinner, stronger, and less easy to attach to the bike. Well, two out of three isn't bad, but the third has turned out to be somewhat of a deal killer. Having to custom-machine your cranks to attach your new pedals has made the sale of his pedals a bit of a niche market. In other words, you've got to really want those pedals or really want to help Dean out to go through all that hassle for such a small part of the bike. Of course, Dean has not been fazed a bit by it and has already developed an updated design with the same necessary crank modification. He is very thick-skinned, which probably comes from being turned down by the large number of the women he has tried to pick up. Don't get me wrong; I truly believe that Dean will come up with a bike design or bike-part-related design that will revolutionize the sport or the mountain bike. But I may be delusional, and I always try to see the best in people while making fun of them, the world, and myself.

Chewy was another Mountain Bike Heaven mechanic. He is a dread-head, looks the part of a gnarly mountain biker, and thrives solely on the mountain bike culture of bikes, drugs, and babes. He is an exceptional rider, crazier than most, and a competent mechanic to boot. Most mountain bike mechanics are quite exceptional riders, with myself being the exception to the rule. Chewy's love for biking is all about riding and racing and partying with other riders, the camaraderie that surrounds the sport. One thing that is true about most mountain bike mechanics is that their bike is usually broken and that's why they generally have a few around. In Chewy's case, it's not uncommon for him to buy someone's relatively unridden, used mountain bike just so that he has one that works.

Over the years, most of the mechanics at Mountain Bike Heaven were real characters. If they had one similar trait, it was a love of bikes. In Canadian Dave's case, it was the love of the mechanics of how the bike worked. This became a bit tedious to some of us, myself included, because we didn't really care how they worked; we just wanted our bike to work. Dave, on the other hand, would study charts and graphs related to how differing suspension types ramped up and made a real science out of it. He would literally spend hours getting a bike's suspension to work at its maximum potential. I can recall many a ride where we would be waiting for Dave to get his own bike suspension set in the field by adjusting a knob or adding air to his shock before he was satisfied with its performance. None of our bikes ever worked that well, and if they had, we probably wouldn't even have known the difference. Many of the riders and most of the mechanics made fun of Dave's technical fetish, but as the years have gone by, I have begun to recognize that it was just what he loved most about the mountain bike. It is not something that I could do or even understand, but it truly is a love, and on the current Sedona mountain bike shop scene, it is quite obvious that Dave is one of the few that loves bikes for what they are rather than for the dollar signs they represent. I, on the other hand, always loved what bikes represent: freedom and the connection to the inner child. Not that I've always remembered that. The other reason Dave got scoffed by the other mechanics and some mountain bikers was that he is just too clean-cut to fit the image of what a true mountain biker represents. Nowadays, I stop by Dave's Fat Tire Bikes and we talk a lot about the philosophy of mountain bike business and the occasional politics of Sedona mountain biking and the world in general.

Windsurfer is an aberration for Sedona. He is a conservative Republican, one of the few allowed in Sedona. He is also one of the most prodigious trail developers and enhancers that had ever landed in Sedona. I knew the moment he arrived that one day trouble would ensue from his efforts, and just recently it has occurred. He came from California, and people that come from Cali have a whole different opinion of what a trail should be. To say this another way, California is not the Wild West which is what Sedona used to be; it is the Yuppie West, full of the beautiful people type. Don't get me wrong; Sedona wouldn't be what it is today without the huge effort of the Windsurfer types, and the trail system is light years better because of their phenomenal vision. Piecing together incredible routes in some of Sedona's gnarliest rocky, cactus-ridden terrain, and opening up unused areas for mountain biker and hiker use, is a vision all trail users can believe in. Of course, the forest circus vision is something different and generally doesn't include having to get out of their trucks. When Windsurfer first came to Sedona, he notoriously wimpified many obstacles that us old timers took pride in riding or not riding depending upon the particular day. We chose to keep them as obstacles to challenge ourselves and others. We were not accustomed to riding every inch of every trail, and

I personally looked forward to those super techy places on the trail that separated the men from the boys.

One place that really pissed me off was the last obstacle on Upper Snake trail. There used to be a small uphill ledge just at the top of the climb that was always a spoiler. You had to climb and climb and climb, and just when you were about to reach the top, you had to make a techy move to clean it all. One day, Windsurfer dumbed it down so everyone could make it. And, if that wasn't bad enough, a few weeks later, he discovered another route that became dubbed the California bypass and bypassed the obstacle completely. We used to take great pride in getting up that obstacle, and if we missed, we went back and gave it another shot. I don't think he did it intentionally to piss me off, but he might have. After all, I'm a bleeding heart liberal and sometimes those right-wingers do things just to piss us liberals off. The reality was, Windsurfer just wanted more people to enjoy the trails without having to struggle and get off their bike and hike-a-bike. I, on the other hand, got great satisfaction from making riders struggle a little or a lot on the trail. A bit topsy-turvy when you think of the current political dichotomy between liberals and conservatives. Nowadays, most of my old struggly routes have been dumbed down or have become overgrown from lack of use, but some still exist and they are still the favorites of us old timers. But, I hate to say this, we have all grown older and even though we call ourselves gnarly old dudes, we are definitely less gnarly, so even I tend to chose the route of least resistance these days.

Gale is perhaps the only one of the crew who grew up in Sedona. He literally knows every nook and cranny of the

Red Rocks whether there is a trail out there or not. He has covered almost as much ground as Max the wonder Brittany Spaniel. Like Max, he is an avid hunter and has used it to expand his knowledge of the area. At first glance, Gale is a very unassuming super Nod, but after many years of riding with him, I have grown to respect his riding. On more than a few occasions, I have seen him ride off of or down something that I have chosen to walk. From the other side, as a bike mechanic, I would guess that some of those things he rode off of would have been better to walk. His bike is almost always in need of some tweaking, not that it really bothers him, and while other bikes seem to be easy to repair, Gale's somehow takes on a life of its own.

Just the other day, I was in Dave's Fat Tire Bike shop where he was working on Gale's brand new bike and, as I said, a simple repair turned into a time-consuming troubleshooting adventure. Of course, while they were trying to fix his bike, I immediately chimed in by saying that's Gale's bike and it would be simplest just to replace the part. BTW, that is exactly what they ended up doing after spending way too much time sorting out the problem. Sometimes you just need to accept that some of the Sedona mountain bikes and riders defy common sense, in more ways than one.

Over the years, Gale has turned into one of the most prodigious trail developers in town. In order not to place his feats in jeopardy, I'll just say there are a bunch of areas that have become everyday rides for Sedonans that wouldn't have been there without his efforts. In addition, there is one area in particular that he has had an ongoing battle with a homeowner to keep open. The homeowner tries to obliterate the trail and in no time at all, it mysteriously gets fixed and the mountain bikers are back riding and having fun. I always have felt that the forest circus and other trail users resented mountain bikers because we obviously have a lot more fun in the woods whether we are riding, hike-a-biking, or enhancing trails. The reality in Sedona is that there is no stopping the mountain bikers and we are not going away, so it is much easier to join in the fun. And, after twenty-plus years of harshing our shred, it appears that the forest circus have finally heard that message and have begun to accept the inevitable, albeit kicking and screaming the whole time like little children.

Plumber Phil, another veteran of Sedona and trail developer extraordinaire, had a different approach to the whole scene. He felt that getting into bed with the forest circus might just be the best alternative. It's not like what it sounds—yes, it is. He began dating the best person the forest circus has ever had in Sedona. I'm not sure how much he talks in his sleep, but the end result has been very effective and he has been able to consult in great detail about issues related to trail development and mountain bikers. Not that the forest circus actually listens to him, but at times they pretend to. It also gives us an inside ear when the forest circus over-maintains a section of trail, which is every time they do trail work. In Sedona, trail maintenance is perceived as a sport. It's all for the benefit of the maintainers, not for the benefit of the trail or the forest as a resource. This is witnessed by the fact that there is always more maintenance performed closer to the parking lots than there is further away, whether it is needed or not. Plumber Phil keeps things very quiet when he's developing trails on his own. It took him almost three years to put in one of Sedona's most amazing trails, and he kept it a secret for most of the time.

The list of riders and friends could go on forever, and it may do just that in another book. So, in order to give respect where respect is due and to leave something for that next book, I have created a list for honorable mention. All these riders, and many more, have helped make Sedona what it is today: Retro George, Wes, Alane, JuliaDear, Eden, Franny, Kevin, Heather, Hulk, Art, Fast Girl, Johnny, Hard Time, Rob Gnarly, Gitty, Laura, Josh, Gabe, Stefan, Janet, Garro, Richard, Wheelie, Long Tall, Dan Diaz, my two adopted daughters Cat and Vanessa, and the guy that hung around until he earned his nickname, The Talking Dude.

I'd also like to add a special thanks to the many mountain bike celebrities who have passed through Sedona: Joe Murray, Richard Cunningham, John Tomac, Henrick Djernis, Tom Richey, Thomas Frischknecht, Cedric Gracia, Anne Caroline Chausson, Brian Lopes, Ross Shnell, Andrew Shandro, Thomas Vanderham, Wade Simmons, Nino Schurter, Florian Vogel, Tinker Juarez, Aaron Chase, JHK, Willow Korber, Shonny Vanlanderham, Elka Brutsaert, Shaums March, Bruce Spicer, and Wade Bootes. Just to mention a few. I'd also like to thank the many Canadian visitors that have come and gone. You guys and gals are the best, and kept me in business for years. There are many names I have forgotten. Don't take it personally; it's been many years and tons of weed that has clouded my memory. Thanks for sharing the good times and the good rides. I wouldn't be writing this book without you.

www.ingramcontent.com/pod-product-compliance
Lightning Source LLC
Chambersburg PA
CBHW031653040426
42453CB00006B/288